WOMEN IN THE EYES OF JESUS

Women in the Eyes of Jesus

Yesterday, Today and Forever

Antoine E. Nachef, STD

ST PAULS

Alba House

New Testament citations are from *The New Testament: St. Paul Catholic Edition* (ST PAULS / Alba House, 2000).

Library of Congress Cataloging-in-Publication Data

Nachef, Antoine, 1967-
  Women in the eyes of Jesus: yesterday, today and forever / Antoine E. Nachef.
      p. cm.
Includes bibliographical references.
  ISBN 0-8189-0947-1
1. Jesus Christ—Views on women. I. Title.

  BT590.W6N33 2003
  226'.0922'082—dc21

                          2003008507

Produced and designed in the United States of America by the
Fathers and Brothers of the Society of St. Paul,
2187 Victory Boulevard, Staten Island, New York 10314-6603,
as part of their communications apostolate.

ISBN: 0-8189-0947-1

Printing Information:

Current Printing - first digit	1	2	3	4	5	6	7	8	9	10

Year of Current Printing - first year shown

2004	2005	2006	2007	2008	2009	2010	2011	2012	2013

DEDICATED TO
St. Peter-Marian Jr.-Sr. High School
Worcester, Massachusetts

Biblical Abbreviations

OLD TESTAMENT

Genesis	Gn	Nehemiah	Ne	Baruch	Ba
Exodus	Ex	Tobit	Tb	Ezekiel	Ezk
Leviticus	Lv	Judith	Jdt	Daniel	Dn
Numbers	Nb	Esther	Est	Hosea	Ho
Deuteronomy	Dt	1 Maccabees	1 M	Joel	Jl
Joshua	Jos	2 Maccabees	2 M	Amos	Am
Judges	Jg	Job	Jb	Obadiah	Ob
Ruth	Rt	Psalms	Ps	Jonah	Jon
1 Samuel	1 S	Proverbs	Pr	Micah	Mi
2 Samuel	2 S	Ecclesiastes	Ec	Nahum	Na
1 Kings	1 K	Song of Songs	Sg	Habakkuk	Hab
2 Kings	2 K	Wisdom	Ws	Zephaniah	Zp
1 Chronicles	1 Ch	Sirach	Si	Haggai	Hg
2 Chronicles	2 Ch	Isaiah	Is	Malachi	Ml
Ezra	Ezr	Jeremiah	Jr	Zechariah	Zc
		Lamentations	Lm		

NEW TESTAMENT

Matthew	Mt	Ephesians	Eph	Hebrews	Heb
Mark	Mk	Philippians	Ph	James	Jm
Luke	Lk	Colossians	Col	1 Peter	1 P
John	Jn	1 Thessalonians	1 Th	2 Peter	2 P
Acts	Ac	2 Thessalonians	2 Th	1 John	1 Jn
Romans	Rm	1 Timothy	1 Tm	2 John	2 Jn
1 Corinthians	1 Cor	2 Timothy	2 Tm	3 John	3 Jn
2 Corinthians	2 Cor	Titus	Tt	Jude	Jude
Galatians	Gal	Philemon	Phm	Revelation	Rv

Table of Contents

Introduction

An Irish Catholic woman thought it is unnecessary to write a book on the lofty dignity and special role of women as defined by Jesus in the Gospels. "If women enjoy an untouchable dignity," she argued, "why should you talk about something that is so obvious? It will reduce its importance because it will look like you are trying to fix something that does not need to be fixed."

Although I think that the Irish woman has a point, women, despite the many improvements in today's world, are still suffering abuse and oppression. Often they are not as respected and appreciated as they ought to be, and their contribution to the quality of life in our society is frequently overlooked. No matter how many programs there are to promote the dignity of women, I don't believe that society values women in the full and authentic sense of the word.

In 1976, the Congregation for the Doctrine of the Faith commented on the presence of women in the human family: "The Church desires that Christian women should become fully aware of the greatness of their mission: today their role is of capital importance both for the renewal and humanization of society and for the rediscovery by believers of the true face of the Church."[1]

Pope John Paul II proclaimed March 12, 2000, a "Day of Pardon." He invited the Church to be sorry for all the sins of her past, and in one section of his prayer he says: "Let us pray for all those who have suffered offenses against their human dignity and whose rights have been trampled; let us pray for women, who are all too often humiliated and emarginated, and let us acknowledge the forms of acquiescence in these sins of which Christians too have been guilty."[2]

The present book does not intend to defend the dignity of women, because their dignity, bestowed on them by God Himself, is already inviolable. Instead, the author wants to highlight the way Jesus upholds the dignity of women. It is interesting to see how He goes against the customs of His society to reveal what God thinks about women. There is a lot to be said about women and Jesus in the surprising number of times that the Lord interacts with women.

Despite the fact that society today is to be commended for its advances toward preserving and improving the dignity of women, an examination of Jesus' relationships and interactions with women will help us to organize and deepen our thoughts on this vital subject. Let us take a look at Holy Scripture and see what Jesus, our ultimate teacher, wants us to learn.

Even though many may think that there is not enough material to produce an entire book on the relationship between women and Jesus, I think differently. Women were heavily involved in Jesus' ministry. He healed them and welcomed their faith. He opened conversations with them and changed their lives. In fact, the longest conversation Jesus ever had in the Gospel was a conversation with a woman. Jesus was interested in the life of each and every woman He encountered. Women supported and provided for Him during His earthly ministry. He appreciated their strong belief in Him since they accepted Him more readily than most men. Women followed Him on the way of the Cross and were the first to witness His Resurrection from the dead.

Every word and every conversation Jesus had with a woman will be studied in this work. One should not take lightly the importance of Jesus' message to the women with whom He interacted. It is the word of God addressed through Jesus to all women of all generations. The timelessness of His message will be analyzed from the social, cultural, theological, and scientific points of view.

A variety of studies on women have recently been completed in the field of religion. Theologians are constantly arguing about the nature of women's role in the community of the Church. Some are extreme in their thoughts to the point of fanatic feminism; others are still undervaluing the essential presence of woman leadership in the Church. In order to avoid both extremes, I propose here to go back to the roots, to the Scriptures. A thorough analysis of women in the Gospels will be of great interest to those who want to know what Jesus Himself thought of women.

My approach seeks to be a balanced analysis of the social, cultural, spiritual, and theological dimensions of Jesus' encounter with women. Every scene in which Jesus interacts with women will be studied from these points of view. The implications of the Gospel vision of women's ultimate role in the world today make up the conclusion of each scene.

Since ancient times, women have been neglected by men and society in general. They have been looked upon as inferior creatures, unjustly despised, mistreated, and harshly misjudged. When we review the history of the world, we realize the great sufferings women have endured down through the ages. Today, society rightly condemns all negative attitudes and actions taken against women in the past. However, after centuries of abuse, we still have to deal with the same problem: how to value the identity and place of women in the life of the human family and society as a whole.

At the dawn of the third millennium, women are still experiencing discrimination in many parts of the world. Sometimes it seems that even progress and technology are unable to change society's view on women. In the most advanced countries, you still hear: "It's just a woman," or, "Don't worry, the opinions of women never count." Politicians often advocate the cause of women in their speeches, but that is as far as it goes. At the very core of our society, women still suffer misunderstanding and low esteem. Aware of this situation, the Second Vatican Council (1962-1965) said: "At present women are involved in nearly all spheres of life: they ought to be permitted to play their part fully according to their own particular nature. It is up to everyone to see to it that woman's specific and necessary participation in cultural life be acknowledged and fostered."[3]

Why do we still have these ideas about women? If they are human creatures just like men, why have they been discriminated against? Do people truly believe that men and women are equal? What is the meaning of this equality? Are women treated in certain institutions better than others?

This book does not dwell on the negative aspects of men's attitude towards women in the past. Rather, it seeks to build a healthy picture of the important place women should occupy in the present world. The third millennium is a time to start taking seriously the role women play in the course of human events. Thinking positively, we will focus more on what they do rather than on what they should not or cannot do. Pope John Paul II comments in his famous document on the dignity and vocation of women: "By defending the dignity of women and their vocation, the Church has shown honor and gratitude for those women who — faithful to the Gospel — have shared in every age in the apostolic mission of the whole People of God. They are the holy martyrs, virgins, and mothers of families, who bravely bore witness to their faith and passed on the Church's faith and tradition by bringing up their children in the spirit of the Gospel."[4]

From the beginning of Christianity, women have played a significant role in the Church, some according to the customs of the times and others in sharp contrast to the conventions of their day. In the New Testament, women are actively involved in the life of Jesus and the early community of the Church. In Jesus' religious and social milieu, males occupied the center of attention; however, Jesus Himself welcomed women and treated them just like men.

Women had a great deal of dignity in the eyes of Jesus and were considered in no way inferior to men.

In Jesus' time, women's public appearance was restricted to certain areas, like drawing water from the local well, shopping in the marketplace, and praying in the synagogue. The idea of women going wherever they please was completely unthinkable in Jesus' society and culture. Despite those restrictions, women frequently appeared in Jesus' company during His public ministry. When we read the Gospel today, we do not appreciate what it meant for women to interact with men in public places. Such freedom was not deemed appropriate for women during the time of Jesus. Women back then normally lived a life of relative seclusion.

Many ancient cultures considered women "impure," meaning that they were unfit to offer proper worship to God. Just because they were women, they were often viewed as inferior to men, sometimes even as property. Traces of that were evident in the Old Testament. Only with the coming of the Lord Jesus did the role of women begin to break new ground, opening up new possibilities for their fulfillment.

Jesus did not always call the kind of disciples that people expected. For one thing, Jesus invited many women to follow Him. This public fellowship between Jesus and women was the ultimate scandal in the eyes and minds of many. The Lord associated with women, He was willing to teach them and treat them as partners. In a society that assumed women should be "seen and not heard," this was quite radical.[5]

Jesus is not physically present to the women of today to give His opinion and be heard by the masses, but He is active in the hearts of the spiritually minded. Empowered by the inner strength that is synonymous with knowing Jesus, women can overcome many of the obstacles they face in today's society. The best way of reaching that goal is studying the Scriptures. What does God's word say to women? We will explore the answer in detail now.

Notes

1. Congregation for the Doctrine of the Faith, Declaration *Inter Insigniores*, no. 6: AAS 69 (1977), 115-116.

2. *L'Osservatore Romano*, March 22, 2000. No. 12 (1635): 4.

3. Vatican II, *Gaudium et Spes* (Church in the Modern World), 60.

4. Pope John Paul II, Apostolic Letter *Mulieris Dignitatem*, no. 27: AAS 80 (1988), 1719.

5. See Marilyn Gustin, *Discovering God's Word*, California: Benziger Publishing Company, 1995, 190-191.

CHAPTER ONE

The Originality of Mark's Gospel:
Special Encounters Between Women and the Divine

Introduction

The author of the first Gospel was John Mark (Ac 12:12 and 25; 13:5-13; 15:37-39; Col 4:10; 2 Tm 4:11). He was Saint Peter's co-worker (1 P 5:13) and companion and probably obtained much specific information from Peter the chief Apostle to write his version of Jesus' story. Mark wrote his Gospel around the year 65 A.D. to a Christian community in Rome that was being persecuted by the Emperor, Nero. An atmosphere of impending persecution pervades the Gospel of Mark.[1]

Compared to Luke, Matthew, and John, Mark's Gospel is the shortest, yet the most original. It draws a vivid picture of the person and mission of Jesus. Mark is like one who goes around at a party and takes snapshots of different events. Later on, he puts them together with a brief narration. Although short and not detail-oriented, Mark's story nevertheless reflects a highly authentic version of what took place in the final three years of Jesus' life.

Saint Mark highlights the power of Jesus revealed in both word and action. Jesus' works and miracles strengthen His words and confirm the authenticity of His teachings. Every word and every action that Jesus performs reflects God's action in human affairs. The divine is fully revealed through the very life of Jesus Christ. Saint Mark calls the revelation of God's presence and action in and through Jesus "Good News," or "Gospel."

The authority of Jesus, however, will be fully revealed through His suffering and death. Dying is not a denial of Jesus' authority; it is part of it. God's logic is different from ours since God shows, through Jesus, that death, freely accepted, is the way God accomplishes victory: the Resurrection. Suffering with and for the sake of Jesus becomes a sign of power because that was God's way of revealing it. Writing to the persecuted community of Rome, Mark reminds them that the death of the Lord, just like theirs, is not merely another sign of weakness. It is a revelation of power and authority. This logic is very hard for those who do not yet have the faith to understand.

The focus of Saint Mark's theology is on the kingdom of God. In His person and His work, Jesus Christ inaugurates God's reign and invites people to follow Him as King of kings. In the person of Christ the definitive display of God's lordship is to be acknowledged by all creation. Belonging to Jesus' kingdom, however, entails trials, suffering and constant battle. The call to discipleship is an invitation to be "with Jesus," sharing His mission of preaching and healing. But Jesus has promised never to leave His followers alone because He is truly the Messiah, the One sent by God Himself, to save humanity and establish God's perpetual kingdom.[2]

One interesting application of Jesus' kingdom theology in Mark is the context in which Jesus deals with women. This is presented not in any lengthy treatise by Mark on God's mission towards women, but simply by reporting the way that Jesus speaks to women and treats them. As simple and brief as are His interchanges with them, Jesus' gentle words and works reveal God's love and respect for women, created equal to men, in God's own image and likeness.

When Saint Mark speaks of women, his presentation of events manifests his own distinct style. He does not worry about details;

he is concerned to present the essence of the meetings between them and Jesus. This underscores Jesus' purpose for interacting with women, His deep appreciation of who they are, and His sincere love and respect for them. In reality, Mark is cleverly telling us that Jesus' words and actions reveal God's words and actions in our history. The humanity of Jesus manifests His divinity because what Jesus humanly does makes the divine present in our world. Jesus' attitude towards women, therefore, is an authentic indication of how God Himself interacts with them. Mark shows that the divine logic is far beyond conventional concepts and that God has inscribed in the being of women a very different image from the one badly misconstrued by male-oriented societies over the ages. Let us take a look now at what was revealed about women in the Gospel of Mark, the earliest Gospel to be written.

A Quick Intervention: Jesus Heals Peter's Mother-in-law
(Mark 1:29-31)

> After leaving the synagogue he went to Simon and Andrew's house with James and John. Peter's mother-in-law was burning with fever, and at once they told Jesus about her. He went over to her, grasped her hand and raised her up, and the fever left her and she began to serve them.[3]

With great power and spontaneity, Jesus miraculously cures Simon Peter's mother-in-law (Mk 1:29-31). Since the Gospel of Mark is the first to be written, this early encounter between Jesus and a sick woman is most interesting. For the first time in the New Testament we see the Lord approaching an ill woman. Most often, being ill in Jesus' time and culture was considered a curse from God. People avoided the sick and considered their affliction a result of

God's punishment. But was Jesus imprisoned by these convictions of His own people? The answer is simple: No. Jesus "went over to her, grasped her hand and raised her up, and the fever left her and she began to serve them" (Mk 1:31).

The encounter between Jesus and Peter's mother-in-law gave a strong message to those who came to know about the miracle. In a society where public physical contact between a man and a woman could evoke a serious scandal, Jesus is not afraid to challenge those customs. Doesn't God's logic transcend human habits and cultural thinking?[4] Wouldn't God show, through Jesus, that He has always been trying to reach out to every human person, man and woman alike, to heal and to save? Isn't the whole human person the very reason why God Himself came down and walked this earth in order to save us?

The short sentence describing the healing of Peter's mother-in-law shows Saint Mark's interest in the concrete actions of Jesus. Jesus does not say anything as He performs the miracle; He just does what He must do. His actions speak louder than any words He could have uttered at that time. The intention of Mark is to highlight the great consequences of Jesus' action: He heals a woman by touching her hand and, through this action, reveals God's love and mercy towards her. But is this short story the end of the message or should it extend to every person throughout history? Not only Peter's mother-in-law, but also every human being who lives, by the story of this biblical woman, is invited to experience God's love and mercy. This love can enter into their lives at a time they least expect.

Right after her miraculous healing, Peter's mother-in-law "began to serve them" (Mk 1:31). Such hospitality was common in the Middle East. During Jesus' time, friends visiting a household were always welcomed with food and drink. Why did Mark mention that "she began to serve them"? The New Testament scholar Daniel Harrington states: "The primary function of this detail (she served them) is to demonstrate the suddenness and completeness of the cure; it is proof of the miraculous nature of Jesus' healing action."[5] Despite the fact that Mark focuses on the suddenness of the cure, the service of Peter's mother-in-law becomes a model for all people of all generations: today, serving the Lord Jesus and being hospitable to His brothers and sisters is an honor and duty for women and men alike.

Women during Jesus' time were known for their hospitality as they received guests and treated them with honor. In turn, women too received honor as their own love and generosity towards guests was reflected in their guests' comfort, gratitude, and pleasure. Taking care of the household in all its detail bestowed on women honor and dignity. Therefore Jesus' healing of Peter's mother-in-law gave her more than a physical healing. He restored her to a role of honor in her family and community.

The situation is different today. Twenty-first century Catholics are sometimes tempted to look with dismay at the way women lived in Jesus' culture. They often project modern thinking patterns on how women should have lived during that time. Even if the culture is different nowadays, God still sees women in the same loving way. Therefore, if today's men and women insist on shaping the culture through their use of modern technology, they should never forget that human nature is still the same as far as being men and women is concerned. They are still finite creatures and depend on Almighty God every step of their way. God's grace, His providential care, and His healing power are necessary for every person to surmount the difficulties of life.

Unfortunately, in the past the contributions of women to the Church have frequently been overlooked because of society's emphasis on their roles as mother, or wife. For instance, Mary Magdalene, although faithful to Jesus to the end, is known more as "the repentant sinner." The Samaritan woman (Jn 4:39) is remembered more for her five husbands than for the fact that many in her town believed in Jesus because of her word. Mary, the Mother of Jesus, is honored for her virginity and motherhood. Only recently, in the Second Vatican Council, were the dimensions of her disciple-ship developed. Mary is not only the virgin-mother of Jesus, but also His disciple par excellence.[6]

How does the healing of Peter's mother-in-law relate to the women of the twenty-first century? Sickness brings us down and creates a crisis in our lives, causing us to experience the frail, lim-ited nature of our human existence. When we are sick, we feel a certain discontinuity in our life: things are not the same and living patterns have to change. We are used to doing things in a certain way. Continuity and habit provided us with a sense of peace be-cause the present seems to predict the future: prosperous and good. When illness knocks on our door, all future plans are challenged and we face a crisis.

Why is there often despair in the heart of the sick person? Because nobody wants to die. We find ourselves strongly attached to our earthly existence. We all want to continue to experience the sense of being alive. Sickness threatens the peace and disturbs a regular and a healthy pace of life. It disrupts our life and challenges our sense of security.

Women tend to be more sensitive and hence often experi-ence this crisis more keenly than men when they are sick. It is not easy for a woman to be sick. Her day to day security is challenged: she cannot fulfill the duties of her state in life as before. The house is a mess, she can't cook or care for her husband and her children as she would like. Even today most women are the primary care givers for their families. When they cannot fulfill that role, they begin to question: Why me? Why doesn't God do something to make my situation easier?

Her sense of self-worth is threatened because illness brings on such a deep sense of insecurity. She is not herself. Normally a giving person, she feels incapable of giving back what she received from God and others. The consequences of this painful experience may result in an existential crisis in which a woman feels she is not good for anything anymore!

By healing Peter's mother-in-law, Jesus shows He understands. He manifests the heart of a loving God Who has healing power, and He directs our attention to a life beyond this world. It is there that our true security lies. Christ gives the answer to all women of all generations: this is how the Lord God cares about women and how He responds when they face a crisis. This woman did not ask for a miracle. Jesus saw her need, healed her and restored her to her family life and happiness. Christ did it because He wants to show the love of the Father towards all women who are suffering. Through the healing of Peter's mother-in-law, Christ imparts hope to all those who are sick.

At the same time, He teaches that there must be a Cross and suffering in this world before one can enter into the fullness of Life and Resurrection. It is only through the Cross that a woman will find the ultimate peace she is looking for. In fact, through the Cross she will find herself relying more on God. She will enter into a closer relationship with Him in prayer, and will then see her heavenly home as the source of her hope and real security. When everything seems to be spinning out of control, Christ intervenes, consoles and redeems. When the ailing woman reaches a point bordering on despair, Christ heals the interior wounds of her heart. He did that for Peter's mother-in-law; He does it for women who are suffering today; He will do it until the end of time.[7]

Women are the True Family of Jesus: They Listen to God's Word and Act on It
(Mark 3:31-35)

His mother came as well as his brothers; they stood outside and sent someone in for him. A crowd was seated around him, and they said to him, "Look, your mother and brothers are outside asking for you." In answer he said to them, "Who are my mother and my

7

brothers?" Then he looked around at those seated in a circle around him and said, "Here are my mother and my brothers. For whoever does the will of God is my brother and sister and mother."[8]

Before analyzing the way Jesus treats His own Mother and His family in this passage, let us take a look at the terms "brothers" and "sisters." During a confrontation with the scribes, people came to Jesus and told Him, "Look, your mother and brothers are outside asking for you" (Mk 3:32). Jesus replies that His mother, brothers, and sisters are those who do the will of God. And as He says this, He points to the crowd gathered around Him to listen to God's word.

In this scene, Jesus speaks about the one true tie that binds the members of a family together. He highlights the thought that, beyond the ties of flesh and blood, the word of God brings people together and enables them to experience the beauty of communion with God. Such a relationship of faith and discipleship is more important than the cultural relationship between blood relatives. In Jesus' culture people belonging to one tribe supported each other, sometimes even at the expense of God's truth. Often, family ties blocked and neglected God's law. On so many occasions, the Ten Commandments and the love of neighbor were ignored because of tribal competitions and issues.[9]

Jesus shows that belonging to God's kingdom is more important than belonging to a clan. By stating that the members of His family are those who listen to God's word, Jesus is not putting His own Mother and His blood relatives down; He is rather elevating the bonds of faith above the bonds of family. Saint Mark's primary interest lies in Christ's attitude towards keeping the word of God above all else. He was describing the important place reserved in the kingdom for those who follow God's word; he was not reporting a disagreement or contradiction between Christ and His family. Nothing in the context of this scene suggests that the Lord, Who citing the Ten Commandments invites us to honor our fathers and mothers, was belittling His Mother Mary and His own family. Mark's intention is clearly to emphasize the supremacy of the bond of faith above all tribal relationships.

The standards of modern Western culture differ from the worldview in Jesus' time. In order to understand Scripture, therefore, we need to travel in our minds to the ancient Holy Land, to the very time and culture of Jesus Christ. Only then can we avoid misreading situations by projecting on Jesus' words and actions our current way of understanding things. In the New Testament, Jesus never despised any person in any way. If Christ forgave the woman sinner and the prostitute, how much more would He treat His own Mother with respect and admiration! For a full treatment of Mary's exalted position in Christianity, I refer you to my two earlier volumes, one of which researches twenty years of Pope John Paul II's teaching on Mary's role in the history of salvation.[10] It is enough to mention that, according to the Word of God, Mary predicts that "behold, henceforth all generations shall call me (Mary) blessed" (Lk 1:48).

How can the story of Jesus' family relate to women of our time? You, as a woman of the twenty-first century, are invited to belong to the family of Jesus. In order to be of His family, you don't have to be His Mother or a member of the tribe of Judah to which as a Jew He belonged. You don't have to be Jewish, i.e., born into the chosen people of Israel. You are a spiritual Israelite by faith.

To be part of Jesus' family means to discover who you are in the eyes of God. Christ invites you to live your own identity as a woman, even though the road to self-fulfillment and self-discovery is sometimes very difficult.[11] Belonging to Christ's family through faith will give you the answer to the mystery of your presence in the universe. Christ alone is able to give you the answer to all the questions you may have about your existence. He works from within you, refreshes your heart, and, in the end, He gives you a share in God's eternal and awesome life. It is a free and open invitation because God's love has been poured out for all the human family without reserve or condition.

When Jesus said that the members of His family are all those who hear the word of God and follow it, He was addressing all people of all generations. His voice still echoes in every church, on every street corner, and in every heart. What a great love Christ has for all women who follow His word every day and act on it![12] What delight He takes in those women who constantly carry the Cross and keep on doing so for the sake of Christ! When Jesus looked about and said that His family consisted of those who listen to His word, He pointed His finger at those surrounding Him. Yet I see this same finger of Jesus, beyond space and time, pointing to every soul that lives out His mystery throughout history. Perhaps He is pointing His finger at you today to make you realize that you have truly belonged to His family all along.

Supernatural Accomplishment: Jesus Raises Jairus' Daughter from the Dead
(Mark 5:21-24 & 35-43)

When Jesus had again crossed over to the other side a large crowd gathered around him, as he stood by the sea. One of the rulers of the synagogue, Jairus by name, came and, when he saw him, fell at his feet and begged him, saying, "My little daughter is dying; please come lay your hands on her and save her life!" So he went off with him. A large crowd was following him and kept crowding in on him.... While he was still speaking some people came from the ruler of the synagogue's household and said, "Your daughter has died; why trouble the teacher further?" But Jesus paid no attention to what was being said and told the ruler of the synagogue, "Don't be afraid; just believe!" And he didn't allow anyone to accompany him except Peter and James and James' brother, John. When they came to the leader of the synagogue's house Jesus saw the confusion and the people weeping and wailing loudly, and when he entered he said to them, "Why are you upset and weeping? The child hasn't died, she's sleeping!" And they just laughed at him. But after driving them all out he took the father of the child and the mother and those who were with him, and he went in to where the child was; and taking hold of the child's hand he said to her, "*Talitha koum*," which, translated, is, "Little girl, I say to you, arise!" At once the little girl got up and began to walk around — she was twelve years old. And at once they were completely overcome with amazement. Then he gave strict orders that no one should know of this and said to give her something to eat.[13]

It is very interesting to know that the first person to be raised from the dead, as reported in the Gospels, is a girl. She is the daughter of Jairus, "one of the rulers of the synagogue" (Mk 5:22). Since Jairus enjoyed this prestigious position, he would receive the respect of all Jewish people. He ranked high in authority, being something like a monsignor or the pastor of a large parish in Capernaum. Because of his position, people were interested in everything he said and did and so they followed him when he went to see Jesus. Jairus said to the Lord: "My little daughter is dying; please come lay your hands on her and save her life!" (Mk 5:23).

Unfortunately, people in Jesus' time and place did not celebrate the birth of a girl as much as they did that of a boy. People considered themselves blessed when a boy was born into a household because he would carry on the family name. There is a saying in the Middle East that one hears even today: "When a girl is born, her problems are born with her." Members of a tribe paid attention much more to a newborn boy than to a newborn girl.

When Jairus asked for the healing of his daughter, it seems that he was aware of Jesus' power because His actions were talked about and were public knowledge. Perhaps he was also aware that Jesus did not discriminate against women at all. Actually, Jesus often reprimanded men who, simply because they were males, considered themselves better than women. Jairus had probably heard that Jesus performed miracles for other women and defended them even when they were considered sinners by the society. Christ healed them physically and spiritually and this fact encouraged Jairus to approach Jesus.

Many children in Jesus' time became sick and there were few cures in those days. The life span then was much shorter and Jairus' daughter was one of those unfortunates who became very sick as a child and was dying. While Jesus was on His way, people from Jairus' house arrived and told him: "Your daughter has died; why trouble the teacher further?" (Mk 5:35). Why would these people make this statement? Either they are not aware of all the miracles Jesus had been performing, or, humanly understandable, they did not believe He could raise someone from the dead. In any case, they interfered by trying to stop Jairus from asking for Jesus' help.

The Evangelist Mark relates: "But Jesus paid no attention to what was being said and told the ruler of the synagogue, 'Don't be afraid; just believe!'" (Mk 5:36). There is a tension here between divine and human logic. Facing human anxiety and the limitations of reason, Jesus shows that divine logic must not be hindered by human thinking that sometimes tends to thwart God's powerful action. In fact, Jesus disregarded the message that the daughter was dead and went to raise her up. When Jesus criticized the commotion and weeping of the people at Jairus' house, they "just laughed at him" (Mk 5:40).

People in the Middle East mourn in a very demonstrative way when a family member or a friend passes away. They cry at length and weep openly. They ceremoniously express their feeling of loss as a way to honor the life of that beloved person. During the time of distress they behave in a dramatic way to show to all their family and friends just how much they are suffering. Sometimes, they push their expression of grief to the limit: it is not unusual for a woman in mourning to throw herself backwards knowing that somebody, thank God, would catch her before she hurt herself. Jesus seems to be criticizing this exaggerated weeping and wailing. The people were acting as if death were an absolute end of life and there was no hope of Resurrection.

When Middle-Eastern people mourn the death of a family member, their friends are supposed to mourn to the same degree. This was how proper respect was shown to the dead person. Trying to stop a person from crying would be offensive. It would be interpreted as keeping the dead person from receiving the honor that was due them. When Jesus criticized the people's conduct at Jairus' house, they were resentful and, feeling certain that the child was dead and not sleeping, they ridiculed Jesus.

Even though Jesus was born into the Jewish culture, His actions, because they reveal God's presence in human history, superseded the bounds of culture. Jesus never let human customs prevent him from doing God's work. Yes, it is good to mourn the dead; but this was not the time or place. Now it was time for human logic to give place to something more. Jesus was "driving them all out" so God's logic could go to work. He entered the room with the father and the mother of the child, took the little girl by the hand and said, in the Aramaic language (the dialect that Jesus spoke), "*'Talitha koum,'* which, translated, is, 'Little girl, I say to you, arise!' At once the little girl got up and began to walk around — she was twelve years old" (Mk 5:41).

"*Talitha koum*" are Jesus' actual brief words raising the girl from the dead. To report them in Aramaic is significant. It shows the authentic character of the incident and its historical veracity. The Gospel of Mark was written thirty years after the death of Jesus, and still the words of Jesus are reported in their original version.

Yes, Jesus raised this girl from the dead by simply saying to her in His own dialect, "arise."

The verb "arise" is similar to the verb used to describe the Resurrection of Jesus. The miracle of raising Jairus' daughter from the dead is a foretaste of Jesus' Resurrection. By this action, Jesus reveals Himself as the Lord of life Who cares about every human being and Who wants all people to rise from the dead. The Resurrection of Jesus is a reality in which both men and women are invited to share. Nothing whatsoever could make the Lord Jesus hesitate to raise that girl from the dead. Though very young, she shares in equal dignity with all men and women of human history in the eyes of God.

Immediately after Jesus raised the girl from the dead "he gave strict orders that no one should know of this and said to give her something to eat" (Mk 5:43). Why would Jesus forbid her mother and father, as well as Peter, John, and James from telling others what had happened? Hadn't the townspeople decided that she was dead? Aren't they now going to see her alive on the streets of their village? Why the secrecy?

A most important theme in the mind of Saint Mark is what scholars today call the "Messianic Secret." Jesus chose to reveal little by little His identity as the expected Messiah. The reason behind this tactic lies in the fact that the people were not yet ready to accept a humble and down-to-earth Messiah. Since the Romans presently occupied the land of the Jews, many of them during the time of Jesus were expecting a military Messiah, a conquering general to liberate them.

In Mark 8:29, Saint Peter confesses Jesus as the Messiah and Jesus orders the Apostles not to tell anyone until He rises from the dead. After the Resurrection of Jesus, the Apostles are empowered by the descent of the Holy Spirit and, only then, are they able to spread this Good News all over the earth.

In the scene where Jesus raises the little girl from the dead, he commands her parents, and Peter, James, and John, not to tell anyone. It is in view of the "Messianic Secret" that we should understand the silence Jesus was imposing. On the other hand, Jesus knew that it was impossible that this news not be spread far and wide, since the people of that village saw the girl dead and now realize that Jesus performed a resurrection miracle. Indeed, Jesus will do the work of His Father no matter what the obstacles are.

The raising of this girl from the dead is not the only occasion on which Jesus leaves people with many unanswered questions. People normally tend to ask questions and expect a prompt answer. But Jesus does not function like that. He invites people to draw their own conclusions based on what they see and hear. If Jesus raised that girl from the dead and knows that people will see her alive again, He must have commanded her parents and the Apostles to keep the secret because He wants the people to think and to draw their own conclusions. This shows how much Jesus respects the freedom of the human person: He invites people to believe in Him; He does not impose faith on them, although faith is a gift of God, in and of itself challenging and imposing.

Another aspect makes the story of Jairus' daughter even more complex. What we are dealing with here is the general resurrection from the dead. Not all of the Jewish people who listened to Jesus and experienced His miracles were ready to accept this belief. In fact, among the Jewish sects, the Sadducees, a group that controlled the affairs of the Temple in Jerusalem, did not believe in the resurrection of the dead. On the other hand, the Pharisees, who were students of the Hebrew Scriptures and highly esteemed teachers of the people, did believe in resurrection. Therefore, Jesus' Jewish audience was itself divided between believers and non-believers in resurrection. By raising the girl from the dead, Jesus also raised many questions in the heart of His audience. The example of Jairus' daughter is evidence of the possibility of resurrection, but the answer to those questions still remains part mystery, part fact. It is a fact because it shows that resurrection is an answer to the mystery of the goal of human existence. It is a mystery because men and women fall short of understanding how Jesus will recreate the human person when he/she dies and leaves this life. Life after death is full of hope and promise, yet clothed in mystery.

But how can this miracle of Jairus' daughter mean something for today's women? What effect can thoughts of resurrection have in their hearts? Resurrection has much to do with the whole human experience of being truly beautiful during this earthly term of life and beyond. The reality is that, despite the best of cosmetics, the human body has been designed by God to age gradually. It might sound cruel to call this to women's attention, but resurrection is the ultimate beauty salon. Thought of it takes us beyond the world of superficial bodily beauty to a deeper reality and a lasting spiritual beauty in God's plan for all of us. Faith in our resurrection from the dead can fill us, even now, with a beauty that surpasses all that external beauty aids could do and preserves the inner person beautiful forever.

The fact that women (as well as men) grow old, creates a real tragedy in the lives of many. Growing old brings along with it a crisis of identity: women change with age and feel that they are not the same any more. They hate it and rightly so. In fact, no one wants to experience the fading of their looks and their health. This crisis that every women experiences has an answer. If you are looking for a long-term solution, Christ gives the answer. He reveals what will happen to all women one day: they will rise beautifully transfigured from the grave.

It is very easy to say that resurrection from the dead is the answer. However, no one can rise without dying. Every woman will have to experience earthly death before enjoying resurrection. But death, as it appears on the surface, negates everything beautiful. Because it is a "death," it takes away temporal pleasure and threatens the continuity of human existence. However, it is because death is the ultimate negation of life that Christ came: that all might have life and have it abundantly. As a negation of death, the ultimate negativity, Christ offers the ultimate answer: life without end. But what woman wants to wait for resurrection in order for her true beauty to be revealed?

Truthfully, faith in resurrection is a very difficult thing to hang on to when one is fully immersed in the things of this world. Yet, Christ shows in Scripture that it is possible and the example of raising Jairus' daughter illustrates the reality of resurrection. Note that this woman was very young to die and perhaps very pretty too. Christ is not against a woman's physical beauty since He created it. It was His very action that made everything beautiful on the face of the earth. At the same time, Christ invites every woman to look at her beauty or external looks as a wonderful gift from God. It is to be admired and recognized. However, it is a problem if a woman's beauty and age becomes the ultimate measure for determining who she is. Christ clearly reveals that resurrection from the dead is the ultimate answer; everything else is just a bridge leading towards the eternal and imperishable beauty of life everlasting.

A Cultural-Shock Miracle: Healing a Woman with a Hemorrhage
(Mark 5:25-34)

Now a woman was there who had had a heavy flow of blood for twelve years and had suffered greatly at the hands of many doctors. She'd spent all she had but had nothing to show for it; on the contrary, her condition was getting worse. Having heard about Jesus, she came with the crowd and touched his cloak from behind, because she said, "If I can just touch part of his clothing, I'll be saved." At once her flow of blood dried up, and she knew in her body that she was cured from the illness. Jesus himself, realizing at once that power had gone out from him, turned around in the crowd and said, "Who touched my clothing?" But his disciples said to him, "You see the crowd pressing in on you! How can you say, 'Who touched me?'" But he kept looking around to see who had done it. So the woman, trembling and afraid because she knew what had happened to her, came and fell down before him and told him the whole truth. Then he said to her, "Daughter, your faith has saved you; go in peace and be cured of your illness."[14]

In Mark 5:25-34, a woman who is suffering from a hemorrhage (a flow of blood) approaches Jesus, hoping to be healed. Doctoring as we know it did not exist in Jesus' time. The practice of medicine was very primitive and many people died because of illnesses that we could easily cure today. Performing a miracle on an incurable illness was quite unexpected and very much appreciated. Many people followed Jesus simply because they knew He was curing all kinds of diseases. This was the case of a woman "who had had a heavy flow of blood for twelve years and had suffered greatly at the hands of many doctors" (Mk 5:25-26).

A woman who is bleeding knows that under Jewish law she is considered impure. She is not to be touched in any way. A man who touches her, even if only accidentally, would immediately become impure himself, and thus not be allowed to worship in the Temple.

During the time of Jesus, Jewish worship was centered on prayers and rituals in the Temple. Not to be able to worship in the Temple implied a total severance of relationship with God. So women during menstruation and at other times when they bled (such as after childbirth) avoided all contact with men.

This woman tried to touch Jesus without being noticed, hoping to be healed by His power. She ignored all the consequences coming from such a contact; she was fixed on her healing more than on any of the cultural implications. Jesus, realizing immediately that someone touched Him, searched for the person. The woman, having been caught, falls down in despair and fear before

Jesus. Instead of reprimanding her, however, Jesus commends her faith and sends her home in peace.

Did the woman touch Jesus because she believed in Him or because she was trying to see if she could be healed? Did she have faith in Jesus or was she curious about His power? Mark reports that "having heard about Jesus, she came with the crowd and touched his cloak from behind, because she said, 'If I can just touch part of his clothing, I'll be saved'" (Mk 5:27-28).

The woman heard about Jesus because His fame was spreading like wildfire all over the Holy Land. She knew that He was healing many people, even those afflicted with serious illnesses. Therefore, she decided to come in contact with Jesus. It was her firm initiative and conviction in Jesus' power that led her to touch Him physically and, consequently, be healed.

Let us analyze this step by step. Why was this woman convinced that she would be healed? She merely heard about Jesus and apparently believed in people's testimonies. Did she have faith in Jesus? In a certain sense, yes. She did take to heart the witness of others who spoke so highly of Him. At the same time, she did not have an educated and informed faith. She simply believed those people who told her about Jesus' miracles. And who would not try to be healed especially if one's situation was so critical?

The extreme condition of this suffering woman encouraged her to take desperate measures. Having no hope of medical assistance, coming to Jesus was the only solution she could see for her problem. The more critical and serious her condition was, the stronger was her faith in the possibility of a healing. After all, she would not lose anything in believing, especially because many who believed before her were in fact healed. That is why she thought: "If I can just touch part of his clothing, I'll be saved" (Mk 5:28).

As one reads the story of this woman in the Bible, it is important not to idealize her faith. It was not a unique, perfect faith. She is just like all people, looking for an answer to her critical situation. At the same time, one cannot deny that she had enough real faith to make it possible for her to receive Jesus' healing touch. She "came with the crowd and touched his cloak from behind" (Mk 5:27). The initiative to touch the Lord physically is the desperate move of someone who has lost every other possible hope.

Immediately after touching the cloak of the Lord, "her flow of blood dried up, and she knew in her body that she was cured from the illness" (Mk 5:29). The answer of Jesus to the initiative of the sick woman is amazing. Without even looking at her or saying anything to her, He healed her. Jesus is so powerful that He heals just by being present and touched. Not only in this instance, but also on many other occasions the Evangelist Mark shows the Lord acting in a "mysterious way." There is a supernatural power coming from Jesus' presence. By being present, Jesus is automatically at work. His very presence radiates energy and accomplishes supernatural healing. Why? Because His very Person, as Saint Mark presents it, inaugurates the healing that the kingdom of God brings to all people. The kingdom of God, far from being a military force (many Jews expected a military Christ who would free them from the power of the Roman Empire), causes peaceful healing and salvation: God is acting in and through the Person of Christ.

Jesus was completely aware that a power of grace had gone out of Him and that someone touched His clothes in a special way (Mk 5:30). He manifests a complete control of what is happening around Him. He knows that a person touched Him differently from all the "crowd pressing in on him" (Mk 5:31). Therefore, the Lord asked: "Who touched my clothing?" (Mk 5:30). Despite the fact that the Apostles told Him that it is crowded and many have accidentally touched Him, Jesus insisted that a power of healing has gone out of Him toward someone special. Jesus "kept looking around to see who had done it" (Mk 5:32), and revealed that something in the sick woman's intention was different from the touch of the pressing crowd. We do not know whether other sick people were present that day; we only know that the scene focuses on this one woman who was healed.

The sick woman took the initiative to touch Jesus hoping to be healed. Jesus' power takes care of her situation and reveals His positive response to her and all those who approach Him with faith. However, Jesus wanted to know who the recipient of His healing touch was. He looked for the woman trying to identify her. Once the identification was made public and the Apostles knew who it was who had touched Him and been healed, the woman approached Jesus again. This time, she feared that Jesus would be upset with her. Her fear comes from her "audacity" in touching a man publicly and also from the fact that she did not openly ask Jesus for a miracle. Having been caught, she "fell down before him and told him the whole truth" (Mk 5:33).

The situation of this woman is similar to that of many women of today's world. How many women do you know who are afraid to approach Jesus just because there is a crowd that tries to prevent them from getting closer to Him? How many walls are erected between Jesus and the needy simply because some people think they have an exclusive right to the Lord and keep everybody else from touching Him? Are we a channel that leads to Jesus or, when we get close to Him, do we try to prevent others from experiencing Him?

It is so easy to categorize others and then judge them. When a religious person feels close to Jesus, his or her trickiest temptation is to start telling others what to do and how to live. Sometimes, sinners are identified and judged by those who call themselves "religious." But did Christ come to save the lost sheep or to save the "saved"? Doesn't He want to lead to His Father especially those who are deprived of His grace and those who are being led astray in this world? It requires a heroic attitude to abstain from judging others and accept those we might presume to be inferior. If we want to be followers of Jesus, we have to be different: the standards by which Jesus acts are radically challenging.[15]

In the most public way, Jesus shows His love and care for the sick woman and for all women who need Him. No crowd should ever try to keep Jesus from looking around to identify a woman who touched Him because she needs to be healed. No people should ever try to monopolize Jesus since He cares about all races and genders. He cures male and female alike. No matter how crowded it is around Him, He knows who is trying to touch Him and He knows who needs healing. He has performed miracles, He is continually performing them all over the world, and He will continue to touch with His divine power every person who approaches Him with faith.

"Daughter, your faith has saved you; go in peace and be cured of your illness" (Mk 5:34), is Jesus' final answer to the sick woman. Actually, these are the only words He spoke to her. The miracle of healing had taken place without any word from Him, a fact that emphasizes more its supernatural character. His message has been communicated through action. Now is the time for His words: to confirm His action. Today, Jesus speaks to women and shows that their faith is the basis for curing, peace, and salvation.

When Jesus healed the woman, He mentioned faith, peace, and salvation. This wording is quite common with Jesus because He does not do anything unless it is somehow related to peace in this world and to eternal salvation. These two components are essential to following the Lord. Peace is a gift that reflects God's presence in our lives and in the world. This peace, however, is authentic only when it leads to eternal salvation. The message of Jesus should never be disconnected from God's eternal life which all people are invited to share. It is a serious mistake to think that Jesus came just to bring us peace and to show us how to live in this world. His message is mainly oriented to an eternity with Him, the Father, the Holy Spirit, and all the saints. Salvation starts here on earth but continues on in an eternity of life and love. The cured woman was invited by Jesus to realize that eternal salvation is at the root of His action.

By healing the woman in a public way, Jesus showed that the limiting customs of His society cannot control His actions.[16] Jesus looks at the value and benefit of people as surpassing all human laws, cultures, and traditions. God loves and wants to heal every person regardless of cultural or social status. In every contact with people, Jesus grants peace, healing, joy, love, and salvation. Let people know what Jesus is able to do in their lives! If every person realized his or her value in the eyes of Jesus, they would rush to Him, their only fountain of life and salvation, and touch Him.

If you hear your friends claiming to "know" what Jesus is all about and still refusing to accept Him, be patient with them. Be patient with them as Jesus is patient with you. Wasn't the sick woman suffering for a long time before Jesus came into her life to change it forever? Before Jesus' healing intervention didn't He wait patiently to show to her God's mysterious ways? You are the hands, the feet, and the heart of Jesus in this world and He relies on your work to extend His healing power to every person you meet. If you are hurting and have never tried before to approach the Lord, it could not hurt to try. You will find an inexhaustible treasure of love and healing there.

Jesus Challenges His Society and Heals the Daughter of a Pagan Woman
(Mark 7:24-30)

After departing from there he went off to the regions of Tyre. He entered a house and didn't want anyone to find out, but he couldn't hide; instead, a woman whose daughter had an unclean spirit heard about him at once and fell at his feet. The woman was a Greek, a Syrophoenician by birth, and she kept begging him to drive the demon out of her daughter. And he said to her, "Let the children be fed first — it isn't right to take the children's bread and throw it to the pups." But she answered and said to him, "Lord, even the pups beneath the table eat the children's crumbs." Then he said to her,

23

"Because of what you've said, go your way; the demon has come out of your daughter." And when she went off to her house, she found the child lying on the bed, and the demon gone.[17]

The focus of Jesus' contact with women before this incident has been on physical and spiritual healing. All the women He cured so far have been of Jewish descent. In the story of the Syrophoenician woman, a different situation arises. Now Jesus is dealing with a non-Jewish woman who is asking for her daughter's healing. Phoenicia is actually Lebanon, a small and beautiful country visited often by King Solomon, son of King David. The Old Testament records that Solomon had unlawful affairs with several Phoenician women and also built his Temple in Jerusalem using the famous cedars of Lebanon. Phoenicia seems to have had a rather bad influence on the religion of the Jews; many times God warns against the corruption of His Covenant people due to the influence of the Phoenician gods. Jesus, in the present case, was dealing with "a Greek, a Syrophoenician by birth" (Mk 7:26).

A pious Jew in Jesus' society was not allowed to associate with pagans. Since pagans did not worship the God of Israel as their own god, Jews considered them impure and unworthy. They were not people of the Covenant and did not enjoy the privileges of the special relationship between God and His chosen ones. A Jew who associated with a pagan would be considered ritually unworthy of praying in the Temple. But Jesus universally "emphasized the dignity and the vocation of women, without conforming to the prevailing customs and to the traditions sanctioned by the legislation of the time."[18]

Far away from the noisy city of Jerusalem, in the district of Tyre, in the southern part of Lebanon, Jesus was seeking some rest: "He entered a house and didn't want anyone to find out, but he couldn't hide" (Mk 7:24). People were nosy in Jesus' world because they wanted to know everything about everybody. There was not much privacy for Him because everybody knew everybody. Jesus, having performed miracles, could not go anywhere without being noticed. It was very hard for Him to take some private retreat time away from the crowds that often intruded on His daily life. He suffered a plight not unlike that of today's celebrities. People were constantly curious about His every move and what He was going to do next.

Apart from His disciples (cf. Mt 15:23), no Jews accompanied Him on his visit to Lebanon. A pagan woman asked Jesus for a favor, putting Him on the spot. I am sure that two immediate problems arose in the minds of those watching: she is not a Jew and she is a woman. Since in Jesus' culture, people are immediately classified, it is important who you are in people's eyes and opinions. It is a society based strictly on honor and shame. Who you are determines what you can do. Asking for a miracle means questioning the extent of Jesus' authority. Is He willing to do a miracle for a non-Jew? For a woman? Is He allowed to do either? Would He treat her with the same respect as He would treat a man?

The daughter of the pagan woman was not with her when the mother came to Jesus. All we know is that her daughter "had an unclean spirit" (Mk 7:25). In our language today we might say that she is "possessed by a demon." "An unclean spirit" indicates, according to scholars, that there was an external force controlling her actions. Not only is it a physical or mental "illness," but also an alien presence opposing God's presence and action.[19] This is not the first time Jesus encounters Satan and demons in the Gospel of Mark. Jesus cured a man possessed by an evil spirit in the very first chapter of the Gospel. He drives out demons because the kingdom of God is present in His person. In any case, what we know for sure is that the Lebanese woman's daughter was not in a normal condition and her mother obviously could not do anything about it.

The fact that the woman came and fell at Jesus' feet (Mk 7:25) indicates that she knew that Jesus was capable of performing a miracle. Because of the considerable tension between Jews and pagans in Jesus' day, prostrating oneself in front of a Jewish man was not common. Jews and pagans did not mix because Jews thought they would become ritually unclean if they were to be touched by pagans. Since the woman's act of prostrating would look very strange and drastically inappropriate, her gesture indicates that she was desperate for a healing miracle. She had clearly stated her needs and "she kept begging him to drive the demon out of her daughter" (Mk 7:26).

Today, in retrospect, we know that Jesus came to heal and to save all people from the beginning of human history until the end of time. But we should not ignore the historical mission He had received from His Father. He was sent by the Father to fulfill the history of salvation which began with the calling of Abraham and the forming of the Jewish nation as God's chosen people. As the Messiah, He was to reign forever over the Jewish nation. It is easy to understand, therefore, that pagans were hardly ready to accept a Jewish Messiah as the Savior of the world. If He is the promised Savior of the Jewish nation, how do we explain the universal sense in which He came to save all people?

The pagan woman did ask for her daughter's healing, but Jesus wanted to make clear the purpose of His divine mission: He came to fulfill the plan of the Father that started with the Jews. They were considered the children of God in the sense of having a very special historic relationship with Him. In many instances in the Old Testament, God refers to Israel as His "beloved child." Based therefore on that concept, Jesus said to the pagan woman: "Let the children be fed first — it isn't right to take the children's bread and throw it to the pups" (Mk 7:27).

At first glance, it seems that Jesus was calling her and her people "dogs." In today's language it would be an offensive gesture. Here, though, Jesus is saying something else. First of all, dogs are the most faithful of animals. In Jesus' time they often accompanied people on their journeys in order to protect them. They were faithful friends who would never leave their masters in time of danger. Nonetheless, although they protect people and sheep from the attack of wolves, dogs are still animals and can never share equal rank with human beings. In the Middle East, even today, canned dog food is not available in shopping centers. Household pets are fed from the leftovers that people give them at the end of a meal.

Perhaps now we can understand why Jesus, when the pagan woman asked for her daughter's healing, did not offend her by saying: "Let the children be fed first — it isn't right to take the children's bread and throw it to the pups" (Mk 7:27). True, Jesus was sent to fulfill His Father's plan and redeem humanity. But the plan of redemption was starting with the chosen people, the people of Israel. Inviting pagans into Jesus' mission plan needed development, time and tact. Only in this sense did pagans come second and are compared to "dogs" being fed from the children's table. In Jesus' eyes all people are equal; however, Jesus' plan of redemption was following a timetable.

The woman would not give up. She answered: "Lord, even the pups beneath the table eat the children's crumbs" (Mk 7:28). The thinking of this pagan woman is quite logical because she knows that in the Middle East dogs are constantly picking up scraps that fall from peoples' meals. She knows that Jesus is a Jew and thus focused on His mission to His own people, but this does not stop her from insisting on a healing. She agrees with Jesus about His special attention to the Jews to whom He is sent to fulfill God's saving plan; yet, is it not still possible that she could receive a "leftover" healing from the abundance of Jesus' power?

The case here is similar to many Gospel situations in which Jesus is moved by the persistence of someone in need. He is interested in how the will of a person is involved in reacting to His initiatives. We see how Jesus responds to a person's request especially when this person insists on obtaining something from Him. The will of a person is very important in the eyes of Jesus because it demonstrates a real willingness to ask for divine assistance. When a person shows his or her utter dependency on Him, Jesus responds and fulfills the desire of that person. In every encounter between Jesus and people, Jesus always responds to the persistent longing of the human will when it is in harmony with God's will.

Because the pagan woman absolutely insisted on getting Jesus to perform her miracle, Jesus granted her request. He performed the miracle even without being physically present to the sick girl. Jesus said to her: "Because of what you said [that the pups under the table eat the children's crumbs], go your way; the demon has come out of your daughter" (Mk 7:29). By uttering this statement, Jesus cured the woman's daughter. This kind of healing through word alone displays the supernatural power of Jesus. The Lord does not need to be physically present to heal people.

The story of the pagan woman is an outstanding example of Jesus' wider concern for the overall cause of women. Perhaps pride keeps women from asking Jesus for healing. Or they think that if God wants to perform a miracle, God knows their needs and they need not ask. But this is a false assumption. In the Gospel encounters between Jesus and women, He clearly reveals how God responds to those who ask Him to do something. And by their insistence, women show their absolute conviction that God can do for them what they ask.

Women forget that Jesus looks at them in the same exact way He looks at men, that is, as creatures endowed with free will and dignity. Like men, if they need Jesus' grace of healing they must ask for it. For Jesus to intervene in their lives they need to insist on it as the pagan woman did. Asking for help is part of the miracle process. Those seeking a miracle still need to submit their will to the will and plan of Jesus if they want healing to take place. In the eyes of God, women are neither at a special advantage or disadvantage because of their gender. Jesus views women and men in the same way: equally worthy of God's grace.

When a woman is sick, physically or spiritually, it is easy to give up hope. In fact, feelings of despair might lead her to think that perseverance is somehow unattainable. The physically ill woman may be so overcome by her symptoms, her prognosis or her total lack of energy, that she believes she is ineligible to receive the healing power of Jesus. The spiritually ill woman may be so overpowered by mistakes she has made, oppression, or other hardships that she simply does not believe that healing can occur. But this is not what Jesus shows us in the case of the pagan woman. Despite the fact that a "demon" had taken hold of her daughter, Jesus intervened and cured the girl showing that His mission is essentially to heal humanity from the snares of evil, sin, and death. The story of the pagan woman's daughter will repeat itself throughout human history every time a woman asks for healing. No woman should never allow a lack of faith, pride or energy to come between her own well being and the healing power of Jesus.[20]

The Evangelist Mark reports that "when she went off to her house she found the child lying on the bed, and the demon gone" (Mk 7:30). In our materialistic culture, nothing is free. Every gift needs to be matched and every favor expects another in return. But with Jesus every gift is totally free because it is based on God's unconditional love.

Jesus Discusses Some Jewish Convictions that Concern Women: Marriage, Divorce, and Resurrection
(Mark 10:1-12 & 12:18-27)

When he went up from there he went to the region of Judea [and] beyond the Jordan. Once again crowds gathered around him, and again, as was his custom, he taught them. Then the Pharisees came forward and asked him if it's lawful for a husband to put his wife away, testing him. In answer he said to them, "What did Moses command you?" They said, "Moses permitted a husband to write a bill of divorce and put his wife away." Jesus said to them, "He wrote that commandment for you because of the hardness of your heart. But from the beginning of creation, He made them male and female; for this reason a man shall leave his father and mother and be united to his wife, and the two shall become one flesh. So, then, they are no longer two but one flesh. Therefore what God has joined together, let man not separate." In the house the disciples asked him about this again. And he said to them, "Whoever puts his wife away and marries another woman commits adultery against his wife, and if a wife puts her husband away and marries another man, she commits adultery."[21]

Then the Sadducees came to him — those who say there's no resurrection — and they questioned him, saying, "Teacher, Moses wrote for us that if a man's brother should die and leave a wife behind but not leave a child, the brother should take his wife and raise up offspring for his brother. There were seven brothers, and the first took a wife and he died without offspring; and the second took her and died without leaving offspring, and the third likewise; and the seven left no offspring. Last of all the woman died. When they rise at the resurrection whose wife will she be? — all seven brothers had her as wife." Jesus said to them, "Isn't this the reason you go astray, that you understand neither the Scriptures nor the power of God? For when you rise from the dead you neither marry nor are given in marriage, but are like the angels in Heaven. But as for the dead rising, haven't you read in the scroll of Moses, at the passage about the thorn bush, how God spoke to him, and said, I am the God of Abraham and the God of Isaac and the God of Jacob? He's not God of the dead but of the living; you've gone seriously astray."[22]

This passage does not fit the pattern of the others. The others have to do with a Jesus-women relationship, whereas this one treats the relationship between women and their husbands in this life and in the next. In this section we will examine how Jesus' views on the relationship between marriage, divorce, and Resurrection, directly relate to women today.

The question of marriage needs considerable attention because it relates to the daily life of our society.[23] Jesus had something to say about the subject when He faced the questioning of the Jewish authorities. In the presence of a large crowd, the Pharisees, a group of Jewish leaders who are experts in the Law of Moses, asked Jesus "if it's lawful for a husband to put his wife away" (Mk 10:2). Although they asked Jesus this question simply to confuse and embarrass Him (Mk 10:2), He carefully answered them and presented them with God's position on the matter.

In a male-oriented society, men were in complete control of the marriage-divorce situation. Women's opinion did not count at all. A man could leave his wife whenever he wanted. She was merely a victim of her husband's unilateral action. Jesus, knowing that the Pharisees' question was intended to trick Him, asked them: "What did Moses command you?" (Mk 10:3). Jesus wanted the law as given by Moses to be the solid starting point of His argument.

The Pharisees answered, "Moses permitted a husband to write a bill of divorce and put his wife away" (Mk 10:4). Jesus told them, "He wrote that commandment for you because of the hardness of your heart. But from the beginning of creation, He made them male and female; for this reason a man shall leave his father and mother and be united to his wife, and the two shall become one flesh. So, then, they're no longer two but one flesh. Therefore, what God has joined together, let man not separate" (Mk 10:5-9).[24]

This answer of Jesus reveals God's position on the relationship between man and woman in marriage. Is it possible that Moses would write something contradictory to God's law just because of the hardness of the people's hearts? Jesus said that He came not to abolish the Law of Moses but to complete it. This "complete it" also means "perfect it." The Law of Moses leads to the law laid down by Jesus Christ for all generations. The Law of Moses is not wrong; it is incomplete. If it were complete, there would be no need for the coming of Jesus Christ and the Gospel. Besides, God had to work with the Jewish people according to their thinking patterns. It was going to require the Incarnation of His Son Jesus for God to reveal fully the meaning of His eternal law on marriage.

The Jewish people were not ready to accept the fact that, from the beginning, God created human beings as man and woman and that this original unity denotes equality in honor, respect, and dignity. Man and woman were both created by God at the beginning of human history. They were created in such a strong unity that marriage's ideal purpose perfectly reflects that original and insepa- rable unity. The unity between man and woman as intended by God invites man to "leave his father and mother and be united with his wife and the two shall become one flesh" (Mk 10:7-8). God did not intend woman to be an object in man's hands. Man should not take a woman for his wife and then feel free to leave her at his pleasure. In Jesus' opinion, man cannot dispose of his wife and ruin her life by a one-sided decision. God intended woman to be of equal rank and dignity with her husband. Their unity covers all the aspects of their mutual life together.[25]

Since God is the creator of this unity between man and woman, "what God has joined together, let man not separate" (Mk 10:9). Woman is not a mere object or a thing to be disposed of at will. A woman becomes one flesh with her husband. Becoming one flesh includes a total union of all that makes man and woman what they are. It is a union between their bodies and their souls. It is also a union in every aspect of their lives together. It does not matter that people have erroneously interpreted this union throughout the centuries. What matters is Jesus' revelation of what God really thinks of the equality of woman and man.[26]

People who believe that the Catholic Church advocates the cause of men over women, are mistaken. I do not deny that many

Catholics throughout history have joined in the neglect of women's rights to equal dignity. But this is not the teaching of the Catholic Church. There is a difference between the personal opinions of Catholics and the official teaching of the Catholic Church, which seeks the authentic teaching of Christ as handed down to us by the Apostles. This teaching is clear: "Whoever puts his wife away and marries another woman commits adultery against his wife; and if a wife divorces her husband and marries another man, she commits adultery" (Mk 10:11-12).

In that statement Jesus makes clear the equality of man and woman. Not only should a man not divorce his wife, but also a wife should not divorce her husband. Jesus is affirming the woman's capacity for independent action. The question remains, however: Is divorce ever allowed in the Catholic Church? What about the recent granting of annulments?

This book is probably not the perfect place to deal with the subject of marriage annulment. It is helpful nevertheless to mention briefly something about the matter because many people, especially women who are mothers, ask questions like: "How is it possible to annul my marriage when I have five children?" "Are my children illegitimate because my marriage was not valid to start with?" "I got married before a priest in front of many people; how can my marriage be invalid?" "Is my marriage really invalid in the eyes of Jesus?"

These are certainly valid questions, but Catholics need to understand better what Jesus intended marriage to be. Marriage is a sacrament — an outward sign instituted by Christ to give grace. It is the only sacrament that depends on the will of the man and woman who love each other and want to enter into a lifelong relationship of love. Now, various things can invalidate a sacrament. What invalidates the sacrament of the Eucharist, for example, is using apple juice instead of grape wine and cornbread instead of bread made from wheat. If baptism is administered with a liquid different from water, the sacrament will be invalid. Sacraments are actions of the Church and take place within the Church according to the mind of Christ Himself.

A bishop or a priest is the ordinary agent of most of the sacraments. What makes the sacrament of marriage unique is the fact that men and women are the agents who enable the sacrament to take place or not. For a marriage to be valid a man and a woman pledge to love and accept each other unconditionally. In doing so they enter into a covenant to be partners for the rest of their lives. Their love for each other reflects the love of God for His people and the love of Christ for His Church.

A wedding ceremony, no matter how solemn and grand, does not necessarily guarantee that a valid marriage has taken place. One of the partners could be entering the marriage without the kind of informed and authentic consent that is required. Any kind of constraint on the will of one of the partners could likewise make the marriage invalid. Certain mental and physical conditions could impair one or both of the partners' ability to enter into a valid marriage. One of the partners might not be free to marry for a variety of reasons, including the fact that they may still be in a morally and legally binding marriage, etc. In such cases, the Church, acting on behalf of Jesus Christ, has the authority to declare the marriage null and void, i.e., grant an annulment.[27]

There is no doubt that God's intention regarding marriage is that it be a lifelong commitment: "Whoever puts his wife away and marries another woman commits adultery against his wife; and if a wife puts her husband away and marries another man, she commits adultery" (Mk 10:11-12). When a couple enters into a valid sacramental marriage, neither the Church nor any human being can break the tie that binds them to each other.[28] Marriage is for life. It cannot be viewed as a job that one can quit when he or she is tired of it.

It is important to note that even today, despite divorce or separation, these ties last forever, especially when there is a child or children involved. The man and woman may no longer love each other and they may not live in the same household, but they are unmistakably bound as one vis-a-vis their children. As much as some men and women would like to totally dismiss the other from their lives, this is impossible to do. Divorced parents need to remain committed to their children even if, for whatever reasons, their commitments to each other no longer exist. It is with Jesus' help that women can experience the healing that is often necessary after a divorce. Seeking Him especially during such emotional trials can give women the power they need to forgive. With true forgiveness, a woman can eventually come to accept the breakdown of the marriage and the loss of commitment that served as its foundation. With forgiveness a woman can effectively and properly support the commitment that remains between her child or children and their father. This noble act should not be oversimplified. It sometimes requires heroic effort through many trials and tribulations to maintain a working relationship between a divorced woman, her children and their father. Women who rely on Jesus can find great strength while living through the difficulties of divorce. Jesus can be relied upon to provide them with the support they need.

At the time of Jesus — and this is true even today in many parts of the Middle East — marriages were arranged by the couple's parents. Love did not always enter into the equation. What was, and is, important was the will of the man and the woman in choosing to commit themselves for life to each other. You will notice in this passage that Christ did not focus on the will and desire of the man exclusively. The woman has an equal part in the process of deciding to marry. Her freedom is to be respected just as much as the freedom of the man: they choose each other. Both parties have wills that need to be used freely and completely in order to make their union perfect.

Moses wrote to the people of the Old Covenant: "If a man's brother should die, and leave a wife behind but not leave a child, the brother should take his wife and raise up offspring for his brother" (Mk 12:19). It is obvious that the woman had nothing to say about the second marriage. But what if she does not like her husband's brother? She had to marry him because this was the way the tribes of Israel could multiply and continue to exist. If the second brother dies, the third should take her, and so on.

The Sadducees were a group of Jews who controlled the affairs of the Jerusalem Temple and did not believe in the resurrection of the dead. They asked Jesus to which brother should this woman belong after death if seven brothers married her, one after the other dying without giving her children: "When they rise at the resurrection whose wife will she be? — all seven brothers had her as wife" (Mk 12:23).

Jesus answered the Sadducees: "Isn't this the reason you go astray, that you understand neither the Scriptures nor the power of God? For when you rise from the dead you neither marry nor are given in marriage, but are like the angels in Heaven" (Mk 12:24). At first, one might think that Jesus is belittling marriage or suggesting that marriage has nothing to do with heaven. Not so at all.

We saw earlier that Jesus stated that "what God has joined together, let man not separate" (Mk 10:9). Marriage is an institution established by God. Therefore, it is a human and a divine institution at the same time. It is divine because God Himself established it from the beginning of creation. It is also human because man and woman are human beings who live together in the bond of marriage in human society. Sacred Scripture clearly indicates that God is the author of marriage. It is not merely the invention of two people who start living together just because they love each other. The intrinsic structure of marriage is created and willed by God Himself.[29]

In other words, God Himself instituted marriage, so it cannot become a goal in itself. Just like all other human realities, marriage is not an absolute reality. Since only God is absolute, marriage will eventually end on earth and take on heavenly dimensions. Jesus reveals the bond of marriage as part of God's plan but only as a bridge to the world that does not fade away. Marriage is an institution where love and life grow on earth as an expression of God's love and life. Human marriage though, like all human reality, is oriented to eternal life. Eternity does not lessen the importance of marriage; rather, it perfects it. The love between a husband and a wife does not end when they leave this world; it receives new dimensions. In fact, these dimensions are the ultimate expression of God's love for His people and Christ for His Church.

Many ask whether they will continue to love their marital partner in heaven. The answer is affirmative because heaven does not stop love; it leads love to its perfection. In heaven, spouses will love each other to the highest degree. That love will not be sexual or selfish. God will be all in all. Spouses will relate to each other in and through the love of God who will be the source of their mutual communication, love and care. Married couples will bask in the glory of God and, in the Holy Spirit, will enjoy the eternal splendor of Jesus Christ risen from the dead. In contemplating God, Father, Son, and Holy Spirit, their love for each other will reach its perfection because they will love each other still, in and through God.

People who think that loving God in heaven will take away from love of their spouses are mistaken. Loving God does not take away from loving others; it heightens and purifies our love of others. It is impossible to love without God, because God Himself is Love. It is also a mistake to think that not believing in God right now will enable them to love their partners better — that somehow God gets in the way. But God's eternity includes the present, and fills the whole of creation. Nothing can ever exist or love without God's gift of creation and salvation. God maintains everything in existence and bestows on the entire universe His gift of life and love.

Men and women of our time are often mistaken in how they imagine heaven. "What eye has not seen nor ear heard... what God has prepared for those who love Him" (1 Cor 2:9). Heaven is what Christ revealed to us, not what others think of it. Heaven is where the longings of the human heart are completely satisfied. Heaven is where the love between people reaches its climax. Heaven is where the love between man and woman becomes eternal in the eternity of God. In heaven every person will realize how awesome human love is, nourished by God's grace. All persons will recognize that they have an infinite dignity because they were created by God to share His eternity. Every person will know with certainty what God wanted them to be, an individual who possesses the perfect image and likeness of God, not someone who possesses the image of what society has pressured them to be.

Marriage is not the issue in heaven. Love is.

Jesus Appreciates the Contribution of a Poor Widow
(Mark 12:41-44)

Then he took a seat opposite the offering box and watched the crowd toss money into the offering box. Many rich people tossed in a great deal, but when one poor widow came she tossed in two small coppers, that is about a penny. He called his disciples together and said to them, "Amen, I say to you, this poor widow tossed in more than all the others who tossed money into the offering box — they all tossed in from their abundance, but she from her want tossed in all that she had, her whole livelihood."[30]

During Jesus' time women could not be independent. The idea of a woman working to support a household was unthinkable. Men supported their wives and provided all that was necessary for their livelihood. Women worked around the house or in the fields. Without a husband, widows were at the mercy of others in the society which made life very hard for them. The male-dominated society treated widows cruelly. They took advantage of them in many different ways, or else ignored and neglected them altogether.

On the other hand, God has always loved and defended widows. An early Father of the Church, Saint Caesarius of Arles, remarks: "In Sacred Scripture, dearly beloved, widows, orphans, and the poor are frequently mentioned with benediction, as we read in the psalms: 'Blessing I will bless her widow, and I will satisfy her poor with bread....' When you hear all this, understand it as concerning the entire Catholic Church, and concerning all in the holy Church who are good, humble, merciful, just, modest, chaste and sober."[31]

The story of the poor widow's donation is important because it shows how much Jesus cares about the poor and the weak. Never does the Lord come down so hard on the abuses by men of women as He did in this story of the poor widow. Speaking about the scribes, a pious group of men who controlled the affairs of the Temple, Jesus said: "They eat up the houses of widows and say long prayers as a pretense — these will receive the greater condemnation!" (Mk 12:40). This is a very strong statement, especially if one considers how highly the scribes were respected by the society. In a culture where religion shaped the thinking and the behavior of the people, it was very startling to see Jesus attacking such eminent religious leaders.

But if Christ came to save and not to condemn, why does He say that the scribes will "receive the greater condemnation"? This shows above all that Christ is truly upset with them because, under the pretext of praying, they were unjustly burdening such a weak group as the widows. "They eat up the houses of widows" and were taking general advantage of them. They stole their money by charging them for what should have been free services. Jesus came to defend the widows against the scribes and against anyone else of power in that social order.

Since religion counted for everything, the power that the scribes enjoyed was beyond description. People accepted automatically whatever a scribe said and did. Scribes expected their fellow Jews to make generous offerings or donations to the Temple treasury. When Jesus was watching "the crowd toss money into the offering box," many rich "tossed in a great deal" (Mk 12:41). Many contributors did it just to receive praise from the people who were watching them. Nobody except Jesus paid any attention to the poor widow who came and "tossed in two small coppers, that is, about a penny" (Mk 12:42).

Not entirely unlike our own, the society in which Jesus lived classified people by giving them dignity solely based on a person's power, money and prestige. Nobody paid any attention to widows because, having no power and generally very little money, they played no role in the society. They lived at the margins of life. It was an eye-opener for the disciples of Jesus to hear Him declare: "Amen, I say to you, this poor widow tossed in more than all the others who tossed money into the offering box — they all tossed in from their abundance, but she from her want tossed in all that she had, her whole livelihood" (Mk 12:43-44).

How did Jesus know that the rich people contributed from their surplus wealth? He could read their hearts and was well aware of the greed that so often controlled their lives: "It's easier," He once said, "for a camel to go through a needle's eye than for a rich man to enter the kingdom of God" (Mk 10:25). In small villages and even in the cities wealthy people were easily identifiable and everybody was aware of their comfortable situation. The rich, in fact, often tried to draw attention to themselves by flaunting their wealth because they knew how much stock people put in money. They loved the adulation of the crowd and sought opportunities to enhance their image. When they made their donation to the treasury, they did so with a flourish.

Jesus never cared about what other people thought, especially when God's standards were at stake. Here he forcefully points out the sharp contrast between people with money to spare and the widow with her limited resources. Those who were attached to their wealth gave only from their surplus. Even though they gave a lot of money, and much more than the widow, their action was still deficient. Notice that Jesus did not consider their contributions as wrong. He did not condemn their giving, nor did He belittle the validity of their contribution. He just pointed to the fact that beneath the valid contribution of the rich there was a selfish intention that subtracted from the value of their good deed. Watched with envy by the crowd, "they have their full reward" (Mt 6:2).

Jesus saw in the story of the widow an opportunity to demonstrate how God values things. The coins of the widow did not have more value than the donations of the rich people measured in monetary terms. The widow had very little income because her husband/provider was dead. What was important to Jesus was not the amount she gave but her intention in doing so. Her intention was superior because she wanted to give her all to the treasury. Her act was perfect since her good intention was accompanied by the generous contribution of all she had.

Down through the ages, the Church has witnessed the extraordinary generosity of women.[32] They have given their time, service, money, and even their lives for the sake of God's Temple, the Church. It has been very simple for many of them: giving their livelihood for the Church has been for them the obvious thing to do. The Church is theirs and they are the Church. Good and holy women have promoted and preserved the Church in every time and place. The Church could not survive without women.[33]

Modern times bring their own peculiar problems and complications to the women of the Church. Many women today are financially prosperous and independent — single, married, and widows included. This becomes a problem when women accept the worldly notion that their dignity and worth is measured by how much money they have and how much money they spend. It is good that they want to look nice, keep a nice home, and have a decent life with their families. It is dangerous, however, when the entire focus of their life becomes merely that. If money, looking attractive, and having prestige are the only criteria for their measuring their self-worth, they are in deep trouble. In fact, at a certain point, they will have to give it all up, for the world as we know it is passing away. Worldly wealth, prestige and physical attractiveness are gifts from God. Yet, they become valueless the moment they are considered absolutes in themselves.

It's important for today's women, whether they are part of the Church or not, to create a balance in their lives. A balance consists of evaluating things the way they have been established by the wisdom of the Creator. Material wealth and the spiritual life are not mutually exclusive. Wealth is a gift from God. It should be appreciated as such and used for good in a world that is constantly passing away. If a woman works hard and has money, she should be pleased with herself. However, her spiritual life and her relationship with God is what makes her ultimately who she is as a human person. She will enjoy this world even better if she knows where to place her priorities.[34]

A Woman Challenges Jewish Authorities and Publicly Anoints the Head of Jesus
(Mark 14:3-9)

While he was at Bethany, reclining at table in Simon the leper's house, a woman came with an alabaster jar of pure oil of nard, of great value; after breaking the alabaster jar she poured the oil over his head. But there were some there who were indignant and said to themselves, "To what purpose was this waste of oil? It could have been sold for more than three hundred denarii and given to the poor," and they criticized her harshly. But Jesus said, "Let her be! Why are you bothering her? She's done a beautiful thing for me. For the poor you always have with you, and whenever you want you can

42

do good to them, but me you will not always have. She's done what she could; she's anointed my body in advance in preparation for burial. Amen, I say to you, wherever the good news is proclaimed in all the world, what she did will also be told in memory of her."[35]

Jesus often visited Bethany, a village not far from Jerusalem. His friend Lazarus, whom He later raised from the dead, and Lazarus' two sisters, Martha and Mary, lived in Bethany. In one of His frequent visits to the village, while Jesus was "reclining at table in Simon the leper's house, a woman came with an alabaster jar of pure oil of nard, of great value; after breaking the alabaster jar she poured the oil over his head" (Mk 14:3).

It would be very strange for us in the Western world if someone poured oil on our heads as we visited a house. In Jesus' culture, there were unusual ways of expressing welcome and hospitality. One of them was pouring oil or perfume on the guests' heads. Another was washing the feet of the guests either with water or perfumed oil. Men could come in contact only with men, and women with women. A public contact between a man and a woman, even of the slightest kind, would be a serious scandal.

In the case of Jesus, the situation becomes extremely complicated because He is known as a teacher among the Jews. As a religious leader, Jesus was supposed to set the example of not touching or being touched by any woman. However, it is obvious that Jesus did not refuse the woman's initiative of pouring perfumed oil on His head. In fact, her act and His acceptance of it challenged those present: "There were some there who were indignant" (Mk 14:4). Their reasoning was: "'To what purpose was this waste of oil? It could have been sold for more than three hundred denarii and given to the poor,' and they criticized her harshly" (Mk 14:4-5).

If the woman used perfumed oil worth three hundred denarii, her gift was substantial. Her initiative shows a deep appreciation of Jesus' person and work. It is obvious that she either had seen

Jesus in action or heard of Him from others. One thing is sure: nobody would pour such expensive oil on a guest's head unless there was great respect for that guest.

Beside the generous gift that the woman offered to Jesus, she also put aside the common customs of her society. Being a woman, she was not supposed to be as familiar with such an honored public figure as Jesus. She knew very well that her move was going to stir up trouble and start gossip around her small town. Her courage shows one thing: all she cared about was honoring the Lord. Her respect for and faith in Jesus went far beyond any cultural restriction.[36]

The fact that the woman approached Jesus publicly, was problematic for Jesus too. In fact, just before the anointing, Mark reports that "the chief priests and scribes were considering how they could seize Jesus on a pretext and kill him" (Mk 14:1). The Jewish authorities were watching every move Jesus made. Having a woman come in contact with Him in public did not help His case with the authorities at all.

Jesus nevertheless interrupted at that point and boldly remarked: "Let her be! Why are you bothering her? She's done a beautiful thing for me. For the poor you always have with you, and whenever you want you can do good to them, but me you will not always have. She's done what she could; she's anointed my body in advance in preparation for burial. Amen, I say to you, wherever the good news is proclaimed in all the world, what she did will also be told in memory of her" (Mk 14:6-9).

Jesus comes to the defense of this woman who honored Him and points out that His presence in the world is unique. It is true that Jesus is really present today in the poor of the world. However, when He was born of the Virgin Mary, His historic life on earth presented a very special opportunity to actually see Him in the flesh. Only a few people had the privilege of seeing the God-Man Jesus Christ with the eyes of the body. It surely must have been an amazing experience to meet Jesus in such close contact, especially for a woman who found herself strongly defended for her act of respectful welcome by this great religious figure.

Jesus came as a Savior to meet the needs of every human being without exception. His encounter with this woman reflects God's equal and magnanimous love for everyone. He applauded her action and made her aware of her own incomparable dignity.[37] Jesus asked those present not to prevent the woman from pouring perfumed oil on His head because He was going to be on earth for only a short while longer. It was a unique time for the Son of God to receive directly the honor of His people in this way. Did not Jesus say: "He who honors me, honors my Father"? Since that time, we are called to serve Jesus in the person of the poor.

By pouring perfumed oil on Jesus' head, the woman has "anointed my body in advance in preparation for burial." It is obvious that the woman did not know that Jesus' death was imminent. Her action was intended to welcome and honor Him; it was an ordinary gesture of hospitality and generosity. Yet, God used her ordinary gesture in His plan of salvation. Anointing Jesus' head became in fact a sign of His forthcoming burial. God transformed an ordinary act into a symbol of salvation. Therefore, "Wherever the good news is proclaimed in all the world, what she did will also be told in memory of her" (Mk 14:9).

This prophecy of Jesus has been fulfilled since the Gospel has been translated into all the languages of the world and everyone has heard about the action of that woman. A simple historical deed became a work of salvation. God becomes present in history through the simple acts of people. Did Jesus need the perfumed oil of that woman? Of course not. And still He, Who made heaven and earth, in this powerful gesture of humility accepted from a mere creature what He Himself created. Our generous God Who created the universe out of the superabundance of His love accepts a generous token of appreciation in return from one of His creatures.

The story of the woman pouring perfumed oil on the head of Jesus in the Gospel of Mark becomes a pattern for all women of all generations. Every woman serving Jesus is serving others and every woman serving others is serving Jesus. Jesus allowed the woman in the Gospel to honor Him and so He gave the possibility to many other women to honor Him too. This service to Jesus and to others enables every woman to see Jesus in others and to see others in Jesus. The entire human family becomes one in which Jesus embraces everybody. We are present in Jesus and He is present in us.

Women today are invited to confidently move closer to the Lord. The Gospel story of the woman illustrates how caring and accepting Jesus is. Even if you feel that the whole world is against you today, know that Jesus is not and will never be. Despite the gossip that took place in the Gospel about the woman (and might take place in your own life), give Him a chance as that woman did. She approached Him with unconditional love and respect. She did not care what others might say; neither was she afraid of His rejection. How many suffering women need to pour perfumed oil on the head of the Lord! The minute they do that, the perfume will be poured right back on them.

Many women today need to set aside their fears and explore a dimension of life that they have perhaps not experienced before. It is unfortunate that their past experiences of abuse and disrespect sometimes stifle their spirit of adventure. How many women lock themselves from the world because of having been rejected in the past by others! How many give up searching for a more abundant life because of these bad experiences!

Here is Jesus' invitation to all of you: Regardless of your past experiences, allow yourself to open up and enjoy the beautiful life possibilities that God is offering you here and now.[38] And if you are reluctant to give life one more chance, at least invite Jesus to do something about it. Do what the woman did in the Gospel: she approached Jesus and allowed Him to do the rest. If you have never reached out to touch the Lord, give it a try.

Praying to Jesus is like anointing Him with oil. He responds with His Divine blessing and graces if we only ask Him for them.

So many people are hurting today because they have lost their way in life. They have no friends among those they daily see at home or work or school. How can we blame them if they have a hard time believing in true love? They experience indifference, hostility and rejection daily. How can we expect them to have faith when all around them people are discouraging them from believing in God? One thing I know: the love and grace of God will guide them as soon as they realize that they are truly loved. The power of Jesus will reach into the depths of their hearts to give them peace and hope. The fire of the Holy Spirit will elevate their whole being and immerse it in the infinite love of God.

Life offers so many possibilities for all of you, women of today. There is so much depth in God's love and mercy. The grace of Jesus will help you make your first move toward Him. Once the Lord does so, do not resist. Be generous in giving yourself to Jesus because, once you do, you will find your true self in all its splendor and beauty. So many worries can invade your being and cloud your mind. Sometimes life does not make any sense to you. Well, isn't it human to feel like that and to experience the limitations of the human condition? Just keep bringing new perfumed oil to be poured on the head of the Lord!

Compassionate Women Witness the Death of Jesus
(Mark 15:40-41)

There were also women watching from a distance, among them Mary Magdalene and Mary mother of James the younger and Joses, and Salome — they had followed him when he was in Galilee and served him — and many other women who had come up with him to Jerusalem.[39]

When the Roman soldiers laid hands on Jesus and arrested Him, "they all abandoned him and fled" (Mk 14:50). This short statement by the Evangelist Mark emphasizes the tragic character of Jesus' arrest. All the Apostles and the disciples left Jesus at the time He most needed them. This was a moment of total betrayal and darkness.

Saint Peter tried to see what was going to happen to Jesus when he was caught by one of the high priest's maids who asked him whether he knew Jesus. Peter denied it three times and, after fully realizing his cowardice, he left, broke down, and wept bitterly. After Peter's denial, none of the twelve Apostles or the disciples are mentioned as being present at any of the tragic events that followed. Only the Apostle John stood at the foot of the Cross with Mary, the Mother of Jesus.

Unlike the Apostles, when Jesus was crucified, women were there "watching from a distance" (Mk 15:40). It is sad to think that women were the only followers of Jesus who dared to stay at the scene of His crucifixion. In Jesus' society, men were supposed to be known for their courage and leadership. Women were expected to keep quiet and obey. But when Jesus was sentenced, it was the women who had the courage to stay with Him to the end while His male disciples deserted Him at the time of His arrest and disappeared until after His death on the Cross.

Who were the women present during the crucifixion of Jesus? "Among them [were] Mary Magdalene and Mary mother of James the younger and Joses, and Salome — they had followed him when he was in Galilee and served him" (Mk 15:40-41). These women were very close to Jesus. He healed Mary Magdalene and brought her back to a righteous way of life. James and Joses are the cousins of Jesus. Their mother Mary was related to Mary, the Mother of Jesus. By virtue of their close family relationship, it seems that Mary (the mother of James and Joses) may have accompanied her sons and followed Jesus during His public ministry. These women spent their own money on Jesus and His followers. I am sure that they cared for Him in many other little ways so that He could focus fully on serving the kingdom of the Father.

There were also "many other women who had come up with him to Jerusalem" (Mk 15:41). Mary Magdalene and the others were the most eminent figures among the women following Jesus, but there were also others. This means that many women publicly devoted their services to the Lord. It seems that they even left their own towns to follow Jesus and serve Him. In spite of the public disgrace of the Cross, those women were not afraid to show their support for Jesus. There they stood watching the crucifixion, their faith challenged by the most horrible scene. Their presence at that moment explains everything: their attachment to Jesus whom they loved and served was far greater than any social taboo.

It is impossible to measure the courage that these women had following Jesus to His crucifixion. Jesus was publicly humiliated, crowned with thorns, and crucified between two criminals. Anyone seen affiliating with Him, aiding and abetting Him, would be suspect in the eyes of the Jewish and the Roman authorities. As frail as they were, those women were somehow strengthened. God knows what was going on inside of them! What were they feeling? Were they afraid to lose the respect of their friends and neighbors or even their very lives? What was it that gave them courage to stay there at the foot of the Cross? Did they somehow know of Jesus' Resurrection?

Generation after generation women have stood beneath the Cross of Jesus and proclaimed their loyalty to His suffering.[40] History witnesses so many heroic women who did not fear even torture and death for love of Jesus. They looked crazy in the eyes of the world. And today the same voice of Jesus echoes through all of human society calling women to follow Him. His voice is, however, often drowned out by the immediate gratifications and passing pleasures of the world.

Following Jesus today seems odd and quite unattractive to many who look for maximum pleasure and minimum pain in life. Many women are caught up in this deceptive search for wealth, fame, sex, thrills, fun, ease, comfort, drugs and the many temptations of a free society. Concurrently, science and technology are working to eliminate all suffering from human life.[41]

Suffering is a negative reality that human nature rejects. People look at suffering as something to be avoided at all costs or eliminated altogether if possible. Yet in God's logic, suffering, although hurtful in itself, can be a source of salvation when it is transformed by the suffering Christ. Christ has revealed that He is powerful enough to turn suffering into the joy of salvation. On the Cross, Jesus stands as a sign of contradiction. In the scandal and weakness of the Cross He reveals the power of Resurrection and life.

Those who blame God then for the existence of suffering will never find a satisfactory answer. How can they say that God does not care about their suffering, when He Himself suffered more than they? Those who keep rejecting suffering in favor of worldly pleasures and gratifications must know deep down in their hearts that something is missing. What is missing is the logic of God which they have replaced with their own logic.

Modern women are faced with choices far more complex than Jesus' loyal followers.[42] And these choices often revolve around the issue of suffering. Some radically reject suffering and blame God for its existence. They spend their lives pointing a finger at God and at the Church with the excuse that they don't get answers. This is because they are locked up in their own logic; they think they already have enough answers to life's mystery. They must, however, take their thinking to a deeper level. The mystery of God, life, and the world presents many different dilemmas. It cannot be resolved instantly because it is a journey to be lived and experienced in its fullness. Even though this journey entails many difficulties and problems, the women standing beneath the Cross are a comforting model for all suffering women.[43]

A Perpetual Mark on Human History: Women Were the First to Witness Jesus' Resurrection
(Mark 16:1-11)

When the Sabbath was over Mary Magdalene and Mary the mother of James and Salome bought spices so they could go anoint him. And very early in the morning of the first day of the week they came to the tomb when the sun had risen. They were saying to each other, "Who will roll the stone away from the door of the tomb for us?" But when they looked up they saw that the stone had been rolled away, for it was very large. When they went into the tomb they saw a young man seated on the right hand side, dressed in a white robe, and they were astonished. "Don't be alarmed," he said, "you're looking for Jesus the Nazarene who was crucified; he's risen; he's not here; look at the place where they laid him! But go tell his disciples and Peter, 'He's going ahead of you into Galilee; you'll see him there just as he told you.'" Then the women went out and fled the tomb, for trembling and amazement had seized them, and they said nothing to anyone for they were afraid. Now when he rose in the early morning of the first day after the Sabbath he appeared first to Mary Magdalene, from whom he had driven out seven demons. She went to announce it to those who had been with him, who were mourning and weeping; and when they heard that he was alive and had been seen by her they refused to believe.[44]

Sacred Scripture presents a serious challenge when it associates suffering with power and death with Resurrection. For many centuries, the Church has preached the Resurrection as the result of Jesus' shameful death on the Cross. This was the central message of the Good News delivered to us through the Gospel. The

51

essence of the history of salvation consists in the death and Resurrection of Jesus. But how is it possible that death and Resurrection are so closely associated in Scripture? Why does the Bible insist that Jesus' Resurrection is the result of His death on the Cross? What are the effects of this truth on people in general and on women in particular?

If one thinks about death and life in the light of human reason, one realizes that it is a dilemma. In the logic of Christ, death and life remain a dilemma, even though they give the only answer to the mystery of human suffering. Christ's death and Resurrection were not exclusively personal experiences: the women who followed Him experienced them, too.

Jesus rewarded the women who defied society and stood alone beneath the Cross. As a result of their faithfulness, they became the first witnesses of His Resurrection. In telling the Apostles about it, they became apostles to the Twelve Apostles.

Because the sun was setting and the Sabbath about to begin as Jesus was being lowered from the Cross, the women had no time to properly anoint His body. Therefore, "when the Sabbath was over Mary Magdalene and Mary the mother of James and Salome bought spices so they could go anoint him. And very early in the morning of the first day of the week they came to the tomb when the sun had risen" (Mk 16:1-2). Here it should be noted that Jesus was delivered as a criminal into the hands of the Jewish authorities who hung Him on a Cross. During His three hours' suffering on the Cross all the Apostles and disciples left Him, because they were afraid of the authorities, who considered as traitors every person who disapproved of Jesus' death.

It was not safe for the women to go to the tomb to anoint Jesus' body. They took the initiative to approach the tomb on Sunday morning despite all the terrible consequences that could possibly result from their doing so. Women followed Jesus not only during His life and at the time of His crucifixion, but also to the very grave where He was buried. They were His ever-faithful disciples. Mark focuses on the women's faithfulness in their discipleship to Jesus. Not even the tomb was able to keep them from following the Lord.

For Mark, the death and Resurrection of Jesus gives meaning to everything He has done during His life. If Jesus did not die and rise, His miracles and teachings would be like those of any wise teacher who left behind no more than rules and teachings. In the case of Christ, His Resurrection confirms His divinity. If the women were faithful disciples, it made sense that they would follow Him even in this final stage of His ministry: Cross, burial, and Resurrection.

While Apostles and disciples failed to be with Jesus at the most critical moments, the women were there every step of the way. Their presence at Jesus' Resurrection confirms their faithfulness to His person and His work. Their discipleship urged them to be with Jesus unconditionally. How wonderful, and how extraordinary, it is to find women standing right there, at the heart of the mystery of redemption. As true disciples, the women were amazed by the miracles of Jesus. They didn't desert Him during the shame of suffering, so they were privileged to witness the greatest miracle of all, His awesome Resurrection.

The women "were saying to each other, 'Who will roll the stone away from the door of the tomb for us?'" (Mk 16:3). When they arrived at Jesus' burial place, they would need some help to roll back the stone that sealed the grave. Where were the Apostles and the disciples? It is obvious that anointing the dead person's body was going to be the women's task. But were there any big, strong male disciples around to help move the big stone from the tomb's entrance?

Saint Mark is silent about the presence of any male disciple on the site of the Resurrection. The first people to witness the supernatural Resurrection of Jesus Christ were the women. The Gospel of Mark emphasizes the presence of an atmosphere of awe during and after the death of Jesus. It focuses on the tragic and cruel death of Jesus Who did nothing but good to all people in His life on earth. The tragic scene of Jesus' death affected everybody and nobody wanted to be connected with it — nobody, that is, except a few women who insisted on being with Him during His death and even after His burial.

In an atmosphere of tragedy and fear, Mary Magdalene and other women went to the tomb. "But when they looked up they saw that the stone had been rolled away, for it was very large. When they went into the tomb they saw a young man seated on the right hand side, dressed in a white robe, and they were astonished. 'Don't be alarmed,' he said, 'you're looking for Jesus the Nazarene who was crucified; he's risen; he's not here; look at the place where they laid him! But go tell his disciples and Peter, "He's going ahead of you into Galilee; you'll see him there just as he told you."' Then the women went out and fled the tomb, for trembling and amazement had seized them, and they said nothing to anyone for they were afraid" (Mk 16:4-8).

Mark does not say who rolled the big stone from the entrance of Jesus' tomb. Yet, he implies that something supernatural happened because the rolling of the stone is connected with the "young man" who opened a conversation with the women. The young man was not described as an angel, although the fact that he is "dressed in a white robe" implicitly suggests it. In any case, a conversation takes place between a heavenly creature and the women.

The rolling back of the stone, the man dressed with white, and the empty tomb, provide the context for the good news: Jesus is not there; He is risen. The women were already amazed, even before the "angel" said a word to them. The heavenly young man comforted them saying: "Do not be alarmed!" He proclaimed the news of Jesus' supernatural Resurrection focusing on the empty tomb. Jesus is not there, He is risen. "Look at the place where they laid him!"

Both Mary Magdalene and the other women were granted the privilege to be the first to know about the supernatural, historical event of Jesus' Resurrection. Mark reports the event in a simple style indicating that Jesus' Resurrection is, indeed, an historical event. Jesus was risen not only in the heart of those who believed in Him; He was truly, physically risen from the dead. He was in the tomb and now, because He had risen, he was not there anymore. Isn't that what the heavenly young man was telling the women? Jesus is not there anymore; the place where He was laid is empty.

The women were completely amazed because the Resurrection of Jesus was unprecedented. Not even in the Jewish religion was it ever known that a man had risen, transfigured, from the dead. There were a few cases of someone being restored to life who, thereafter, died again. And there was the mysterious case of the prophet Elijah who was assumed into heaven by a fiery chariot and never seen again. But the event of Jesus' Resurrection was totally unexpected by everyone, even by those who had heard Him predict it during His public ministry.

The angel did not make the situation easy for the women to understand. He told them not to be amazed, and he complicated matters even further by saying to them: "You're looking for Jesus the Nazarene who was crucified; he's risen; he's not here." Mark points to a harmonious continuity between the crucified and the risen Jesus. The same Jesus, whom they saw on the Cross is now risen from the dead. What was the effect of Jesus' Resurrection of these women? An early Father of the Church, Saint Peter Chrysologus, says in this regard: "The women entered the tomb to become sharers of His (Jesus') burial and companions of His sufferings. They departed from the tomb that they might arise in their faith before they should arise again in their bodies."[45]

Mark's reader should keep in mind that this Gospel was addressed to a persecuted community of Christians in Rome. The Good News of salvation invites this community not to lose heart as its members face suffering for the sake of their faith. Suffering and joy, death and Resurrection, are two dimensions of the same mystery. It is by suffering and dying that Christians in Rome, just like their Lord Jesus in Jerusalem, would conquer death and embrace eternal life.[46]

The women knew from the "young man" that their Lord was

not there anymore and something supernatural had happened. They were commissioned by him to go and tell the disciples and Peter to go to Galilee. It was an honor for them to witness the Resurrection of Jesus Christ before Peter and the other disciples. Peter, who confessed Jesus as the Messiah at the culminating point of Saint Mark's Gospel (Mk 8:27-29), now receives the Good News from women. These women became the first apostles ever to announce the Resurrection of Jesus. Just think of it! The first person ever to proclaim the Resurrection of Jesus Christ in the Church was a woman: "When he rose in the early morning of the first day after the Sabbath he appeared first to Mary Magdalene.... [and] she went to announce it to those who had been with him" (Mk 16:9-10). What a privilege and what an awesome example to follow!

There was a specific reason that Jesus wanted Mary Magdalene and the other women to announce the Good News of His Resurrection to Peter and the other Apostles. He knew He could depend on them. The very mission of the Church to preach the Resurrection started with the extraordinary experience of simple women who had the courage to follow Jesus even through the shame of the Cross. As a result they were given the privilege of experiencing the Resurrection and becoming apostles to the Twelve Apostles.

That doesn't mean it was easy for them. Not only was the death of Jesus on the Cross a difficult experience, His Resurrection was also frightening. "The women went out and fled the tomb, for trembling and amazement had seized them and they said nothing to anyone because they were afraid." It was not usual to hear of a person alive after experiencing a horrible death. The fact that Jesus was proclaimed alive by the "young man," brought nothing but confusion to the women who did not expect to come upon a situation of such magnitude.

Women standing witness in the Church today, carry on in history what Mary Magdalene and the other women did two thousand years ago: they preach the Resurrection of Jesus Christ. Every woman who proclaims Jesus' Resurrection shares, in a certain sense, in the mission of those women. How beautiful is women's mission in our Church today! At the very beginning of the Church's life, there emerged women who, despite their fear and confusion, announced the empty tomb to the disciples. Today, women continue to spread the Good News of eternal life.

Every woman is a bearer of Jesus' Good News because, at the beginning of the Church and down through all of human history, women have shown the world what it means to have faith.[47] The power of Jesus' Resurrection has encouraged thousands of women to give their whole lives in service of the Risen Lord. Many of them have a true vocation to spread the Good News of Jesus' Resurrection and are not even aware of it. Christ is certainly speaking to them, probably not through a heavenly creature, like the angel. But Christ speaks to them through the people with whom they interact every day. The responsibility can, of course, be very challenging. Yet, the love of Jesus will never cease to support them as they seek to fulfill their role in the history of salvation.[48]

Conclusion in Light of Jesus' Resurrection: The Body as the Most Concrete Dimension of the Human Person's Existence

We have treated several biblical themes that involve women in the Gospel of Saint Mark. Jesus heals Peter's mother-in-law and others. Women are capable of hearing the Word of God and of following it. Jesus raises Jairus' daughter from the dead and answers questions regarding marriage and eternal life. Women change their lives and show unconditional generosity and service. They have the necessary courage and faithfulness to follow Jesus even to His death on the Cross. Women enjoyed the exclusive privilege of being the first to witness the Resurrection of Jesus Christ.

While women apply any or all of these themes to their lives

today, the key to doing so is a complete appreciation for what their life means. In this world they live, move, and exist in a human body. Therefore, the relationship between women and the world necessarily involves the reality of their bodies. The body is not what human nature is all about. There is also a soul united to the body from the first moment of a person's existence. The ultimate goal of the human person's life is the resurrection of both body and soul at the end of time.

The Resurrection of Jesus reaches the human nature of every human being, men and women alike. In light of it, let us consider how people can better understand the reality of their own bodies. The body is in fact the first thing a human person is aware of. The human body is the most concrete sign of subjectivity. Persons become aware of their existence as human subjects through their experience of the body.

It is human nature to seek love, happiness, and comfort. Women especially look for love. As an integral part of their feminine subjectivity, they feel the need to be accepted and respected by others. At the same time, women have an awesome capacity to love and to offer themselves to others in fulfillment of their various vocations in life. It is important for them not to mistakenly look for acceptance in the wrong places and from the wrong people.

There is an increasingly widespread acceptance of the spirit of rationalism in our world's understanding of the human body. By analyzing the body as a mere complex of biological tissues, rationalism reduces the human person to its visible dimension, to his or her body. When the spiritual dimension of the body is overlooked, the human person becomes just another animal. But the person cannot be reduced to the body alone and is not identical with the body, because it transcends the body. If man and woman are merely a complex of biological systems, there would be no reason for them not to be exploited by science and society. Essentially, rationalism overlooks the fact that the body of the human person is united to a spiritual soul and that both together make up one reality: the human person. The body should never be seen as a separate entity in and by itself.[49]

Every person, as an inseparable combination of body and soul, is made in the image and likeness of God. The human person is a unified totality whose nature is both corporeal and spiritual. Both the visible body and the invisible soul are brought together in the being of the person. Because man and woman are persons in a unity of body and soul, the soul is embodied and the body is spiritualized.[50]

One of rationalism's influences on our world is the excessive care human beings give to things and to animals. It is true that God created things and animals to be our companions and we, as rational beings, should respect their place in our world. Their existence demonstrates the greatness of the Creator who gave them as a gift to humankind. The place of animals in the world, however, is restricted to being animals.

Since the beginning of the universe's existence God made all creation for the sake of men and women. They alone enjoy the prerogative of being made in the image and likeness of God. All creatures are made for men and women who alone are destined for God's eternity. Therefore, the body of the human person is different from the body of the animal because animals do not have a spiritual soul and neither were they created in the image and likeness of God.[51] Therefore, like all other creatures, they will not rise from the dead.

Resurrection from the dead is the exclusive prerogative of the human person. Only our bodies will receive the glory of the Resurrection on the last day. At the end of time, that is when human history ceases to exist, all people will rise from the dead. Each and every person will receive a different degree of glory according to the perfection of being they reached in this life. Only then will men and women fully realize their dignity and the important role their bodies played in this life. God has always invited men and women to realize that their bodies are temples of the Holy Spirit and instruments of salvation. The body, in its union with the soul, makes up the totality of the human person. Therefore, on the last day of the Resurrection, each person's risen body will join his or her soul. In this way the totality of the human person will be saved. God created man and woman as a unity of body and soul, and only as such will they enjoy eternal life with Him forever in heaven.

One might ask what form the risen body will take. The risen body will be a "new creation." In the same way the old body was fashioned by God in the womb of the mother, so also the new body will be fashioned by God. Yet, the new body will receive from God a glorious shape. It is the same body of the same person, even though it is created anew. When the Apostles saw the Risen Christ they were afraid because they saw something supernatural. Our risen body, in the image of Christ's risen body, will experience a sharing in God's glory. Yet, Christ confirmed to the Apostles that it was He who is risen and invited them to look at the places where His body was pierced. This shows that it was the same body of the same Jesus. Consequently, resurrection brings at the same time continuity and discontinuity in the human person. It is continuity because the same person rises from the dead, and discontinuity because resurrection is a "new creation." New creation indicates a new activity of God who gives the new life of the Risen Jesus to every person saved.

Today it is necessary to have a new outlook on the body of the human person. The body is the concrete subjectivity of the person. It is the most concrete sign of the person's existence. Therefore, even after death, a person's body symbolizes what that person was, is, and will always be. Because the body will rise from the dead, it should never be abused, harmed, disrespected, or mistreated. Since Christ redeemed the entire human person, body and soul, the body is the creation of God and the temple of the Holy Spirit.

Notes

[1] For more information on the Gospel of Mark, see E. Best, *Mark: The Gospel as Story,* Edinburgh, 1983; Daniel J. Harrington, "The Gospel According to Mark" in *The New Jerome Biblical Commentary,* New Jersey: Prentice Hall, 1990, 596-629.

[2] Daniel J. Harrington, "The Gospel According to Mark" in *The New Jerome Biblical Commentary,* New Jersey: Prentice Hall, 1990, 596-597.

[3] Mk 1:29-31.

[4] See Vatican II, *Gaudium et Spes* (Church in the Modern World), 60.

[5] Daniel J. Harrington, "The Gospel According to Mark" in *The New Jerome Biblical Commentary,* New Jersey: Prentice Hall, 1990, 601.

[6] See Antoine E. Nachef, *Mary's Pope: John Paul II, Mary, and the Church since Vatican II.* WI: Sheed and Ward, 2000; "Women in the Church" in Richard P. McBrien, *Encyclopedia of Catholicism,* San Francisco: HarperCollins, 1995, 1331.

[7] See *Catechism of the Catholic Church*, 489.

[8] Mk 3:31-35.

[9] See Bertrand Buby, *Mary of Galilee. Woman of Israel-Daughter of Zion,* Vol. II, New York: Alba House, 1995, 51-56.

[10] See Antoine E. Nachef, *Mary's Pope: John Paul II, Mary, and the Church since Vatican II,* WI: Sheed and Ward, 2000; *The Faith of Mary,* New York: Alba House, 2002.

[11] See in this regard Pope Paul VI, *Marialis Cultus,* 34 and 37.

[12] See *Catechism of the Catholic Church,* 489.

[13] Mk 6:21-24 and 35-43.

[14] Mk 6:25-34.

[15] See "Women in the Church" in Richard P. McBrien, *Encyclopedia of Catholicism,* San Francisco: HarperCollins, 1995, 1330-1331.

[16] See *Catechism of the Catholic Church*, 489.

[17] Mk 7:24-30.

[18] Pope John Paul II, *Mulieris Dignitatem* (August 15, 1988), no. 26: AAS 80 (1988): 1715.

[19] See Daniel J. Harrington, "The Gospel According to Mark" in *The New Jerome Biblical Commentary,* New Jersey: Prentice Hall, 1990, 602-603.

[20] See *Catechism of the Catholic Church,* 489.

[21] Mk 10:1-12.

[22] Mk 12:18-27.

[23] See *Catechism of the Catholic Church,* 355, 383.

[24] See *Catechism of the Catholic Church,* 355, 383; Pope John Paul II, Apostolic Exhortation *The Lay Members of Christ's Faithful People,* Boston: St. Paul Books & Media, 1988, 136.

[25] See Raniero Cantalamessa, *Virginity. A Positive Approach to Celibacy for the Sake of the Kingdom of Heaven,* New York: Alba House, 1995, 53-55; "Women

in the Church" in Richard P. McBrien, *Encyclopedia of Catholicism,* San Francisco: HarperCollins, 1995, 1330-1331.

[26] See *Catechism of the Catholic Church,* 355, 383; Vatican II, *Gaudium et Spes* (Church in the Modern World), 60.

[27] See *Catechism of the Catholic Church,* 1628, 1629.

[28] See *Catechism of the Catholic Church,* 355, 383.

[29] Ibid.

[30] Mk 12:41-44.

[31] See Saint Caesarius of Arles, Sermon 49, in *The Fathers of the Church,* Vol. 31, New York: Fathers of the Church, Inc., 1956, 250.

[32] See *Catechism of the Catholic Church,* 489.

[33] See Pope John Paul II, Apostolic Exhortation *The Lay Members of Christ's Faithful People,* Boston: St. Paul Books & Media, 1988, 135-137.

[34] See Pope Paul VI, *Marialis Cultus,* 34.

[35] Mk 14:3-9.

[36] See Vatican II, *Gaudium et Spes* (Church in the Modern World), 60.

[37] See *Catechism of the Catholic Church,* 489.

[38] See Vatican II, *Gaudium et Spes* (Church in the Modern World), 60.

[39] Mk 15:40-41. Matthew (27:56) and John (19:25) report that there are *three* women with the Virgin Mary at the Cross! The sister of the mother of Jesus (in John) is Salome (in Mark) or is the mother of Zebedee's sons (in Matthew).

[40] See *Catechism of the Catholic Church,* 489.

[41] See Raniero Cantalamessa, *Virginity. A Positive Approach to Celibacy for the Sake of the Kingdom of Heaven,* New York: Alba House, 1955, 74-84.

[42] See Pope Paul VI, *Marialis Cultus,* 34.

[43] See Saint John of the Cross, *December 14 Breviary reading on Suffering.*

[44] Mk 16:1-11.

[45] See Saint Peter Chrysologus, *Sermon 80,* The Fathers of the Church, Vol. 17, New York: Fathers of the Church, Inc., 1956, 130.

[46] See *Catechism of the Catholic Church,* 2853.

[47] See *Catechism of the Catholic Church,* 489.

[48] See *Catechism of the Catholic Church,* 2853.

[49] See Vatican II, *Gaudium et Spes,* 14.

[50] See Pope John Paul II, *Familiaris Consortio,* 11; *Letter to Families,* 19.

[51] See Congregation for the Doctrine of the Faith, *Donum Vitae* (Instruction on Bioethics), Introduction, 3.

CHAPTER TWO

Saint Luke's Unique Vision:
Women Play a Major Role in the History of Salvation

Introduction

B ible scholars agree that both Saint Luke and Saint Matthew have borrowed much information from the Evangelist Mark for their own theology. Further, the same encounters between Jesus and women that are found in Luke are also found in Matthew. Further still, Saint Luke offers new stories and, as it is well known among theologians, Luke sheds unique light on the role of women in the history of salvation. Therefore, in order to avoid repetition, the present work focuses its analysis on Luke's special insights.

Luke took most of his material from Saint Mark and expressed himself according to his understanding of the person of Jesus and His mission. Many of the scenes concerning women that are in Luke's Gospel are already found in Mark. However, there is something in Luke about the dignity of women that the other Evangelists did not discover. What is it?

Luke was a Syrian from Antioch. He was a physician and a companion and collaborator of Saint Paul. As a master of Greek, he wrote his version of Jesus' Gospel between 80 and 85 A.D. Luke "addresses a primarily Gentile audience with well-to-do members who are painfully rethinking their missionary thrusts in a hostile environment."[1] Luke's Gospel portrays a sense of the internal and external controversies among Jews, Jewish Christians, and Gentile Christians.

Gentiles who converted to Christ had a dilemma: If God has not been faithful to promises He made to His own people, the Jews, and has allowed Jerusalem and the Temple to be destroyed (70 A.D.), what reason do Gentiles have to think that this God will be faithful to promises made to them? The Gospel of Luke, however, demonstrates that God, through Jesus, was and will always be faithful to His people. Yet, in an unexpected way, God's promises include the Gentiles, the unclean, the poor, women, Samaritans, rich toll collectors, outcasts and any and all people who are repentant of their initial rejection of Jesus. Saint Luke tells the Gentile Christians that there is a new Israel to which all are invited, the Church. Without excluding any person, all peoples of the earth are invited to construct this new Israel. In this spirit, at the very beginning of his Gospel, Luke reports that "all flesh shall see the salvation of God" (Lk 3:6).

Luke's Gospel is a journey: Jesus travels to Jerusalem so that, by His death and Resurrection, He might fulfill the Father's promises to all people including the Gentiles. The events of salvation start and end in the Temple of Jerusalem; Jesus' ministry begins and concludes with prayer. This indicates that Saint Luke upholds the validity of the Old Testament and the Jewish law. While Jesus stands in this noble tradition, He forms a new Israel by selecting Twelve Apostles instead of the twelve tribes of Israel.

Those Gentiles who believed in Jesus during Luke's time had to contend with the Jews who had already followed Jesus. These Jews sought to apply overly strict entrance requirements to the Gentiles who wanted to join the reconstituted Israel, the Church. Luke's communities faced harassment from local Jewish synagogue leaders, especially the Pharisees, so he developed Jesus' view of who the true children of Abraham are (Lk 13:10-17 and 19:1-10). The "poor of God," lame, blind, maimed, outcast, and women, all play a role in the new community of the Church. Social status, ethnic heritage, and religious self-justification do not qualify for membership in this group.

The people were wiser than their leaders because many, both Jews and Gentiles, ultimately accepted Jesus. They contemplated the meaning of His crucifixion and repented for their sins. From these repentant sinners, Jesus makes up the new community of the Church. God shows His faithfulness to all the members of this new group, Gentiles as well as Jews, because Jesus is risen from the dead. In turn, they are all invited to spread the Good News to all corners of the globe. At the end they will receive their places at the heavenly banquet with Abraham, Isaac, and Jacob.

This short description of Luke's theology offers us the framework in which we can understand Jesus' attitude, love, and respect towards women. Luke is interested in proclaiming the universality of God's salvation by assuring us that Jesus includes everybody in God's plan of reconstituting Israel by founding the Church. What kind of role do women play in the new community of the Church? How does Jesus interact with them?

Elizabeth: A Woman Filled with the Holy Spirit
(Luke 1:41-45)

Elizabeth is the mother of Saint John the Baptist and the wife of the priest Zechariah. We don't know much about either of them, but we do know that they were "righteous before God, blamelessly following all the commandments and regulations of the Lord" (Lk 1:6). Elizabeth is one of those Jewish women who followed the paths described by God in the Hebrew Scriptures. Like others we have noted before her in the history of Israel, Elizabeth had no child because she "was barren and they were both [she and her husband Zechariah] on in years" (Lk 1:7).

Since the beginning of human existence, procreation has always been inscribed in the very being of all women because it fulfills their longing to "give" life to another human person. This mindset enabled women to share in God's original plan of creation. Through procreation, women perpetuate God's creative activity in the history of our world. Since we believe that God created the human person in the beginning, then we also must believe that God is still creating people with the wonderful cooperation of women. A pregnant woman is not only an instrument of God's plan, but an active agent in the mysterious vocation of motherhood.

Based on this concept of motherhood the Jewish people considered it a disgrace when a woman could not get pregnant. Imagine how much scorn a woman then had to endure from society if she was unable to bear a child. Because the culture during Jesus' time did not care about women's innermost sensitivity, society could be very cruel.

In the same way that God intervened to take away the shame of childlessness from many Jewish women, God also gave Zechariah and Elizabeth the chance to have a child. Children coming from barren wombs have played a significant role in the history of Israel. At the dawn of the New Covenant, John the Baptist emerges as the prophet who was going to prepare for the coming of the Messiah. The special circumstances of his conception clearly indicated that God had a divine mission for him.

After Zechariah's serving time as a priest was over, "Elizabeth became pregnant, and she secluded herself for five months, saying: 'Thus has the Lord dealt with me in the days He deigned to take away my disgrace before men'" (Lk 1:24-25). Saint Luke does not explain why the Lord chose Elizabeth to deliver her from the shame of barrenness. From the description the angel gave to Zechariah we conclude that their son is sent by God to accomplish a mission. His name will be John which means "Yahweh (God of Israel) has shown favor."

In the sixth month of Elizabeth's pregnancy, the angel Gabriel was sent to the Virgin Mary announcing the Incarnation of Jesus in her womb. This book does not analyze in detail the very important role that Mary plays as a key woman in the history of salvation.[2] The focus presently is on Elizabeth. After the Annunciation, Mary set out to visit her cousin Elizabeth who was pregnant with John the Baptist.

Saint Luke reports:

> When Elizabeth heard Mary's greeting the baby leapt in her womb, Elizabeth was filled with the Holy Spirit, and she exclaimed with a loud cry, "Blessed are you among women, and blessed is the fruit of your womb! But how is it that the mother of my Lord should come to *me*? For, behold, when the sound of your greeting came to my ears, the baby in my womb leapt with a great joy. Blessed is she who believed that there would be a fulfillment of what was spoken to her by the Lord."[3]

The encounter between Elizabeth and Mary is an interesting scene to ponder. Here we have two women who, in a very special and unique way, are experiencing God's intervention in their lives and ultimately in the lives of their people. One is carrying John the Baptist and the other is carrying Jesus. John will prepare for the coming of Jesus, and Jesus confirms the mission of John. The encounter between Elizabeth and Mary is reflected in the "interior" encounter between John and Jesus. Six months old, John the Baptist leaps for joy in the womb of Elizabeth as she was filled with the Holy Spirit.

It is well known that Luke emphasizes the role of the Holy Spirit in the people of Israel and in the Church. The descent of the Holy Spirit that enabled Mary to conceive Jesus, is now being confirmed through the words of Elizabeth. The Holy Spirit makes Mary pregnant with Jesus and the same Holy Spirit proclaims, through Elizabeth, that Mary is "the Mother of the Lord."

The expression "Lord" in the Gospel of Luke, incidentally,

means "divine" and "God." The same word used by the Hebrew Scriptures to describe the God of Israel is now applied to Jesus. If Jesus is Lord, Jesus is divine. If Mary is the "Mother of the Lord," Mary is also Mother of God. She is Mother of God because Jesus, Who became a man in her womb, is Lord and God.

Elizabeth, a woman filled with the Holy Spirit, is the first to proclaim Mary as "Mother of the Lord." Later on, in the Ecumenical Council of Ephesus (431 A.D.), Mary was officially proclaimed Mother of God. Thanks to Elizabeth's words, the Church continues to profess Mary as Mother of God and "Mother of the Lord." Being Mother of the Lord was the essential vocation of Mary: what an extraordinary vocation it was to carry God in the flesh in her womb.

None of the women who played a major role in the Old Covenant was ever called "Mother of the Lord." This would have been considered a blasphemy in the eyes of every pious Jew, especially since the expression "Lord" was reserved to God. How could it be possible that God could have a Mother? With the mechanism of the New Covenant, there was a movement from above to below: God assumes human flesh in the womb of Mary and becomes truly and authentically human. The Holy Spirit who made that movement possible is now confirming, through the words of Elizabeth, that Mary is the "Mother of the Lord."

Elizabeth, filled with the Holy Spirit, reveals to us in Scripture that Mary's Motherhood is connected specifically with her faith. Talking to Mary, she says: "For, behold, when the sound of your greeting came to my ears, the baby in my womb leapt with a great joy. Blessed is she who believed that there would be a fulfillment of what was spoken to her by the Lord" (Lk 1:44-45). The faith of Mary, as demonstrated by her belief in the words spoken by the Angel Gabriel, allowed her to become the Mother of the Lord: "Behold, you will conceive in your womb and will bear a son, and you shall name him Jesus" (Lk 1:31). Her acceptance of God's call to this motherhood was a free choice. Yet, God was the One Who called her. The Second Vatican Council (1962-1965), which has put the faith of the Church in terms accessible to modern thinking patterns, beautifully expresses the reality of Mary's motherhood when saying that God predestined her from all ages to become the Mother of His Only Son.

God calls both Elizabeth and Mary to motherhood. They both had a firm faith and accepted God's calling. Mary, having believed in the words of the Angel Gabriel, accepted her role as the Mother of the Lord. Elizabeth secluded herself for five months saying: "Thus has the Lord dealt with me in the days He deigned to take away my disgrace before men" (Lk 1:25). Elizabeth believed that her call to motherhood was the result of divine intervention and that God Himself had performed a miracle in her.

After the conversation between the Angel Gabriel and Zechariah in the vision at the temple, Zechariah was unable to talk. Gabriel told him that he would stay dumb until the birth of his son, John the Baptist. Elizabeth's conception was a source of joy for her neighbors who "rejoiced with her" (Lk 1:58). When the day of circumcision came, they wanted to name the child Zechariah, like his father. Elizabeth insisted that "he shall be called John" (Lk 1:60). But if Zechariah was unable to speak yet, how is it that Elizabeth knew that the child's name should be John? The Scripture does not mention anybody telling her the name that the Angel Gabriel gave to her husband Zechariah. Elizabeth has perhaps also received in a supernatural way information about the destiny and vocation of her son John. Zechariah could also have written "notes" to Elizabeth about the name of his future child just as he wrote on a tablet "His name is John" on the day of John's circumcision (Lk 1:59-63).

The Gospel presents Elizabeth first and foremost as a "righteous" person, even before the Lord granted her wish to become pregnant (Lk 1:6). The righteousness and goodness of Elizabeth does not depend on her motherhood, but on her being a good and faithful person. Every woman is invited here to know that she is a good person not because she has children, but because she is a human being. Jesus Himself did not have children and was not married. Such a state of abstinence and consecration to God is very positive. Indeed, those who renounce marriage "for the sake of the kingdom of heaven" are singled out and praised by Jesus (cf. Mt 19:12).

How can the story of Elizabeth influence the women of today? What is the meaning of Elizabeth's motherhood and in what way does it promote this special vocation and dignity of women? What is motherhood's relationship with faith? The story of Elizabeth is unique because she became the mother of John the Baptist. He is the prophet who was to prepare for the coming of Jesus Christ and the one of whom Jesus later stated, "I say to you, among those born of women none is greater than John [the Baptist]" (Lk 7:28).

Many women cannot become pregnant due to their own or their husband's infertility. Elizabeth is the model for all women who suffer because they want to have children and are unable to do so. It is easier today than in Elizabeth's time for women who do not have children. Back then, it was considered a shame and a disgrace. With the New Covenant, in persons like Mary and Elizabeth, God reaffirms that every woman has unimpeachable dignity, not because of her social status or her capacity to bear children, but simply because she is a human person.

The Gospel of Luke reveals that ultimately what matters is the faith that every woman ought to have in God's plan. This faith is their response to God's will for them in this life. More than any other Evangelist, Saint Luke emphasizes that those women who are poor, sick, living on the margin of society, despised, abused, or forgotten, all have a unique and special place in God's plan.

We live in a very cruel world where much of the time society does not support the success of women. In his 1994 letter to women, Pope John Paul II vehemently attacked the behavior of those men who abuse women and make life unbearable. Now is the time for men to realize the true value of women in the eyes of God. Jesus Christ is their ultimate defender in the arduous trials of life. If women rely on the judgment of society as a measure of their worth, they will often find little to bolster their self-esteem. Our competitive society will leave many feeling unfulfilled. If, however, women seek their dignity and vocation in God's will, they will find happiness forever. It does not matter what this vocation is (be it motherhood, marriage without children, or the single life); what matters is the love with which she fulfills it. She is called to be and to live as a child of God. Her faith and her love constitute the ultimate criteria for fulfilling the deepest longing of her heart.

Every time you see two women pregnant having a conversation, think of Elizabeth and Mary. Remember that their vocation to motherhood brought John the Baptist and Jesus into our broken world. If you are pregnant, remember that your children also have a vocation and that you, as a woman and as a mother, play a major role in nurturing their vocation. Scriptures show that every woman enjoys an unimpeachable dignity before God which no human being or social system can ever take from them.

Anna Waits More than Half a Century for the Coming of the Christ
(Luke 2:36-38)

When Jesus was presented in the Temple, Jesus and Mary met a very special woman, Anna, who had something important to say about the coming of Christ.[4] Saint Luke reports:

> The prophetess Anna was there, too, the daughter of Phanuel from the tribe of Asher; she was greatly advanced in years, having lived seven years with her husband from her virginity and alone as a widow up to eighty-four years, never leaving the Temple and worshipping night and day with fasts and prayer. And she came up at that very hour and began to give thanks to God,

and spoke about him to all who were awaiting the liberation of Israel.[5]

A prophet or prophetess in Scripture is a person who knows
and communicates the will of God to the people. A prophet is not
an individual who, through the use of some kind of magical divina-
tion, predicts the future. Rather, the prophet is a pious person who,
through prayer, keeps in contact with God and so has the capacity
to understand God's will for the people in any given time and place.
It is in the framework of history and culture that the prophet reveals what the people ought to do as they respond to God's call. In
a given specific historical period, the prophet plays the role of in-
termediary between God and the people.

According to Jewish custom, a mother was to be purified in
the Temple forty days after the birth of a son. She was required to
make an offering of a lamb for a burnt offering and of a young pigeon or a turtledove for a sin offering. A poor woman could substitute another pigeon for the lamb. Mary fulfilled this requirement of
the Law, even to the making of the sin offering. Another requirement of the Law was that the firstborn son was to be consecrated
to the Lord and redeemed by the payment of five shekels. Both
events were combined on this occasion. Anna is described as a
prophetess in the Gospel of Luke. In what sense was she a prophetess? In the sense that, at that specific moment in the history of
salvation, Anna revealed to the people in the Temple that Jesus of
Nazareth is the long-awaited Christ. The promise that the God of
Israel made to send Christ was now fulfilled. Anna witnessed and
confirmed the accomplishments of God's will: "And she came up
at that very hour and began to give thanks to God, and spoke about
him to all who were awaiting the liberation of Israel" (Lk 2:38).

In order to stay in touch with God, Anna had been practically
living in the Temple for more than half of a century. After spending seven years with her husband, she became a widow and moved
into the Temple to pray and to live in communion with God: "never

leaving the Temple and worshipping night and day with fasts and prayer" (Lk 2:37). She dedicated her entire existence to wait for the coming of Christ Who was to redeem the people of Israel. The heroic character of this woman shines forth in Scripture and is inscribed in the memory of people forever. Hers was not an easy life: her commitment to wait for Christ over fifty years will be preached wherever the Gospel is proclaimed.

Anna was not a superwoman or a magician. She was a pious Jew who was called by God and given a special mission. She responded positively and dedicated her whole life to the service of the Lord. Can her example speak to today's women? Who today would want to spend her entire life in church praying and fasting? Do the challenges of life in our society leave any room for such a radical commitment?

Many women in the Church today are prophetesses, even though they might not be aware of it. They know the will of God through prayer, sacrifice, and fasting. They are constantly in communion with God and communicate God's will to everyone they meet. Many of them are living a very quiet life of holiness, but their example nevertheless shines forth for those who live around them. For years and years they serve the Church and the people of God, often without being noticed. These are the heroic women of our society who give their entire life to the service of Jesus' Gospel. Just like Anna in Scripture, their eminent example spreads all over the earth.

There are also many women today who are prophetesses and already aware of their role in the Church and in human society. As simple and humble as they are, they are able to transform the normal conditions of our culture into a place where God brings salvation. Through hard work, they are able to change human history into salvation history. And what is salvation history but the presence of God's will and redemptive action in the everyday circumstances of life? Many women, after the example of Anna, have always been bringing into space and time the saving work of God.

How long have women been hoping for the coming of Christ into a certain culture or society? Just like Anna waited over fifty years for that to happen, many women still do the same. Some of them work day and night to infuse Christian values and education into their homes and communities. How many fragile women find themselves in rough neighborhoods praying for Christ to come into the hearts of those among whom they live? And how many women missionaries in faraway places are spreading the Good News of Christ in their service of God's children? It is impossible to adequately describe the hard work and sacrifices those women make for the sake of the Gospel.

The prophetess Anna has become a sister and model for every woman willing to give witness to Christ's presence in history. Because you are a woman, you have a special vocation to wait for Christ's call in your life. Sometimes waiting can become very hard and challenging, but He will eventually come to you. Anna is a model of patience for all those women who are living in the hope of seeing Christ. No matter how long it takes and how challenging it is, Jesus' promise will be fulfilled and women will experience the presence of the Lord in their lives. Instead of visiting the Temple of Jerusalem, Christ will visit the temple of their hearts. And what will be the results? Redemption, love, peace, and courage to proclaim to all people the salvation of God. It is amazing how brightly the fire burns in the hearts of those women who patiently wait for Christ. In an unexpected moment, Christ will fulfill their expectations and reward their perseverance.

Jesus Releases a Widow from Her Deep Sorrow
(Luke 7:11-17)

The Evangelist Luke is the only one who relates Jesus' miracle of raising a widow's son from the dead.

It happened that soon afterwards he [Jesus] went to a city called Nain, and his disciples and a large crowd went with him. Now as he approached the city gate, behold, a dead man was being carried out for burial. He was the only son of his mother, who was a widow, and a considerable crowd from the city was with her. The Lord was moved with pity when he saw her and said, "Don't weep!" Then he went forward and touched the bier and the bearers stood still, and he said, "Young man, I say to you, arise!" Then the dead man sat up and began to speak, and Jesus gave him to his mother. Fear seized them all, and they glorified God, saying, "A great prophet has risen among us! God has visited his people!" And this account of him went out through all Judea and the whole surrounding region.[6]

This story is touching because it describes Jesus' compassion in a very special way. For unknown reasons, Jesus was journeying with His disciples through Nain, a small and insignificant city. Like all famous teachers in Israel, Jesus attracted a large crowd. People in Jesus' society were always waiting for something new and curious to happen.

The scene is very interesting because at the gate of the city, a funeral was taking place. During Jesus' time, a dead person remained at home for a short time to be mourned by the neighbors. After a very intense mourning, the dead person was carried in a coffin and brought to a cemetery. As the people carried the coffin, there was a kind of procession: people walked behind the coffin crying, screaming, and mourning the loss of the loved one. Normally, all the people who knew the dead person would walk from the house to the cemetery as a sign of compassion and solidarity. The dead person's family would be offended if their friends did not walk with them to the cemetery. Consequently, since all people know each other in small towns, this usually involved a sizeable crowd following the coffin to the grave.

When the widow was walking behind the coffin "a considerable crowd from the city was with her" (Lk 7:12). Her husband had already passed away and her only child was now being buried. People in Jesus' culture were family oriented. The loss of a husband created a tragic situation for a woman. Her children would become her only comfort and security. People in that culture were known for saying "the one who brings children into the world, does not die." Before his death, the son of the widow of Nain assumed the role of his dead father. He was the one who protected and cared for his mother through the ups and downs of life. The presence of a son in the life of a mother (especially if she was a widow), was regarded as a blessing and good luck. And now the only hope in the widow's life was gone. Who would protect and provide for her now? If you attended a funeral of a "young man" in Jesus' society, you would be struck at the uncontrollable mourning of the mother. Unquestionably, the widow of Nain was experiencing the most devastating situation one can imagine.

Although the focus of this passage seems to be on Jesus' miraculous action of raising the widow's son from the dead, Jesus interacts with the widow in the most compassionate way. Christ was moved with pity for her. Why? Were funerals of young people so unusual? Why did He choose this young man to raise from the dead? Jesus works in the framework of history and society. He was passing by when the opportunity presented itself: a widow was in deep sorrow and the Lord wanted to do something about it during that specific moment of His activity.

Jesus is the Lord and the One Who, especially in Saint Luke's Gospel, reveals the compassionate attitude of the Father towards humanity. The invitation Jesus addressed to the widow, "Do not weep," is God's invitation to all humanity "not to weep." Why would Jesus invite a widow not to cry, if He knew that her sorrow was almost too deep to be controlled? Further, the society in which she lived was harsh and would despise her if she did not bitterly mourn her son. People would gossip about her insensitivity for a century if she did not rend her garments in the process of mourning her only child. Knowing all that, Jesus still invited her not to weep.

Jesus always challenged the customs of His world especially when they ran counter to God's standards. Crying over the loss of a loved one is part of life; Jesus Himself wept when His friend Lazarus passed away. The problem Jesus sees, however, is when the mourning person cries in such a way that there is no room for hope in resurrection. Jesus does not want to eliminate the sorrow that accompanies death; but He wants to transform it into a new reality. A certain balance should exist between crying at the loss of someone and not forgetting the eternal destiny for which God has created all of us.

Crying, mourning, and being sad goes against every woman's natural inclination to be happy. Women are created to enjoy God's life and love, although they are understandably devastated by the loss of loved ones. Jesus and only Jesus brings hope to every woman's heart when life is challenged in this way. In the midst of sorrow and despair, Jesus intervenes to remedy the most difficult situations. Christ does not function the way society does. Where society expects things to happen in a certain way and at a certain time, Jesus, as in the funeral of the widow's son, unexpectedly intervenes and alters the situation.

Notice that the widow did not ask Jesus to do anything about the death of her son. She may well have heard that Jesus was passing through her town because such a special occasion would never pass unnoticed in Jesus' time. In most of the healings we have analyzed up to now, it seems that Jesus expects people to ask for a miracle. What makes this miracle more special is the fact that the woman did not take the initiative to ask for healing. Human initiative would show the absolute dependence people have on God's grace and help. In this widow's situation it is different: Jesus acts out of divine compassion and shows the attitude of a loving Father towards human suffering. God cares about the pain of the human family and, during such tragic occasions, does not need to be asked to sympathize.

Jesus' words to the widow of Nain, "Don't weep," represent God's ultimate invitation to every grieving woman: Do not cry because God is a life-giving Being stronger than death itself. For many generations women have cried because life is very hard on them. Loneliness, despair, death, the breaking of relationships, fear, anxiety, uncertain future, sickness and many other problems have afflicted women of all cultures and all times. How many of them were aware of the power Christ could have brought to their lives? How many ever heard Him say: "Don't weep"?

It is very difficult sometimes to be quiet and realize that Jesus is aware and doing something about our problems, that we are not left all alone to try to cope. The dilemma is that Jesus often helps and heals according to God's plan and not according to what we think God should do. In any case, the presence of Jesus will alleviate the situation. As He did for the widow of Nain, He will come forward to comfort our hearts without even being asked to intervene.

In the midst of their suffering, women often don't feel that Jesus is present when they need Him. Here we must separate the world of feeling from the world of reality. What someone feels is not necessarily what is truly going on. For reasons known only to God, our human limitations are such that we do not always feel Jesus' action in our lives. In the midst of turmoil, sadness, and despair, somehow Jesus is present in a way only known to Him. No woman, though, has ever hoped for the intervention of Christ and been denied.

After Jesus raised the widow's son from the dead, He "gave him to his mother" (Lk 7:15). Imagine Jesus, God in the flesh, encountering a sorrowful widow and handing her dead son back to her alive! Jesus wants every woman to have her children alive in her household. But how can this be applied to all those families who have lost their children and don't have them anymore? How can one console a woman who does not have at her side a child she cherished more than anything in the whole universe? The answer is this: resurrection.

Although life is very hard for those families who have endured the loss of a child, they must not fall into despair. No one can imagine the pain a mother feels in such a situation. She has the right to be sad and even go through human "doubts" about the meaning of existence. Jesus understands why these women may seem to question their faith. Why has such a tragedy happened to them? There are no suitable answers that can alleviate their pain. What can we say to a woman who sees her only child in a coffin? No words are ever sufficient to comfort her. Yet, through the overall picture of despair, there shines forth the answer Jesus provides: resurrection from the dead.

Jesus raised the widow's son to reveal to all people of all times that resurrection is God's answer to the tragedy of human death. The widow's son becomes the model for all those who are looking for an answer to the dilemma of suffering and death.

The hardest part of it all, as Jesus reveals in the Gospels, is the fact that the answer is not quick enough for our fast-paced society. We want immediate answers for all the problems that emerge in daily life. We want things to be resolved right away. But God does not function that way. God's way of doing things is therefore upsetting for many who try to impose their own method and time on God's way of acting. Resurrection, although it includes the negative experience of dying, represents God's ultimate offer of everlasting life to every person. It is for the sole purpose of having life in its fullness that God created men and women in His own image and likeness. This fullness is expressed through the awesome mystery of resurrection from the dead.

Against All Hope, Jesus Pardons a Sinful Woman
(Luke 7:36-50)

In the Gospels we have many stories of forgiveness. Jesus encounters men and women and changes their lives by revealing the
Father's deep love for them. The common reaction of healed sinners is amazement at God's unconditional commitment to forgive
sins.

Saint Luke relates:

Now one of the Pharisees asked Jesus to eat with him,
so he went into the Pharisee's house and reclined at
table. There was a woman who was a sinner in the city,
and when she learned that "he's reclining at table in the
Pharisee's house!" she bought an alabaster jar of perfumed oil and stood behind by his feet, weeping, and
began to wet his feet with her tears and to wipe them
with the hair of her head, and she kissed his feet repeatedly, and anointed them with the oil. When the Pharisee who had invited him saw this he said to himself, "If
this fellow were a prophet, he'd realize who and what
kind of woman it is who's touching him — she's a sinner!" Jesus said to him, "Simon, I have something to
say to you!" "Speak, Teacher," he said. "Two men were
debtors of a certain moneylender; the one owed five hundred denarii, the other, fifty. When they were unable to
repay, he forgave them both. Which of them, then, will
love him more?" In reply, Simon said, "I suppose the
one he forgave the most." "You've judged correctly,"
he said. Then turning to the woman he said to Simon,
"You see this woman? I came into your house — you
gave me no water for my feet, but she wet my feet with
her tears and dried them with her hair. You gave me no
kisses, but she, from the moment she came in, has not

stopped kissing my feet. You didn't anoint my head with olive oil, but she anointed my feet with perfumed oil. Therefore I tell you: her sins, many as they are, have been forgiven, and so she has shown great love. But whoever is forgiven little, loves little." Then he said to her, "Your sins are forgiven." And those reclining at table began to say to themselves, "Who is this fellow who even forgives sins?" Then he said to the woman, "Your faith has saved you, go in peace!"[7]

This story of Saint Luke is similar to one we find in Saint Mark, Saint Matthew and Saint John about a woman who came to anoint Jesus with perfumed oil. There are some important differences in Saint Luke, though, that we do not find in the other Gospel accounts. Luke presents the woman as a "sinner" who not only put ointment on Jesus' feet, but also bathed them with her tears, wiped them with her hair, and kissed them. Jesus' forgiveness of her many sins was measured by the love she poured out. He also praised the quality of her faith, which brought her peace and salvation.

As a teacher among the Jewish people, Jesus was invited by one of the Jewish leaders, Simon, to dine with him. It is obvious that the family and friends of Simon the Pharisee were also present. In fact, it was a custom in Jesus' time to invite all one's friends and relatives to their house when a prominent figure was to be an invited guest. I am sure that many Pharisees were watching what Jesus was saying and doing (see Lk 7:49). The dinner seems to have been semi-public: Jesus was reclining at table eating and several Jewish leaders and friends of Simon were present with Him.

Because the news of Jesus' presence spread like wild fire, a "sinful" woman learned that Jesus was eating at the house of Simon. In what sense was this woman "sinful" and why is she described like that? She was not necessarily more sinful than the men whose sins Jesus had forgiven. The point is the "categorizing" of people in Jesus' society. Jesus never judged people according to society's standards and He certainly never categorized them. In fact, Jesus Himself once attacked those men full of pride stating that "tax collectors and prostitutes are entering the kingdom of God" (Mt 21:31) before them.

Saint Luke does not describe the woman as a "sinner" as a sign of disrespect. He was reporting how people looked at her. She was probably a prostitute who sold her body to make a living. She is one of those people who were silently enduring the pressure of life and society, just to be able to survive. If she was a sinner, weren't all those who were sleeping with her also sinners? In fact, they were probably more responsible for making her a "sinner" than she was.

How often, in Jesus' culture and our own, men commit serious sins without assuming responsibility for their actions. Men have often taken advantage of the fact that they dominated the society in which they lived, and at times, have literally gotten away with murder. Yet, they arrange to look good to others so that they would continue being respected. Jesus harshly attacked such hypocrisy on many occasions and showed that God sees everything and judges the hearts, intentions, and actions of everyone.

Beyond doubt, this woman put Jesus in a socially embarrassing situation by bathing His feet with her tears, kissing them, and drying them with her hair. It took a lot of courage for her to ignore all the customs of her time and touch a Jewish teacher publicly. Only God knows what was happening inside of her. It was her repentant and contrite heart that moved her to approach the Lord. This woman represents a burdened humanity trying to get close to Jesus in order to receive from Him the healing and peace it so desires. Once convinced that Jesus is the only remedy for her situation, no human custom or habit could ever stop her from touching the body of Jesus Christ.

In the eyes of Simon the Pharisee her behavior was scandalous because she was publicly known as a "sinner." The thoughts of Simon irked Jesus; they vividly showed that Simon, a leader of the Jewish people, had forgotten God's mercy. Didn't God constantly forgive the Jewish people on many occasions after they had turned their backs on Him?

Jesus teaches Simon a very simple lesson by means of a parable. Two people owe a master a certain amount of money and the master forgives them the debt. Which one will like him more, the one who owed the master more or the one who owed him less? Of course, the one who owed him more will love him more. So it is with the woman: she loves Jesus more than Simon because Jesus forgave her more than He forgave Simon.

Notice that Jesus is not attacking the good life or the good actions of Simon the Pharisee. Jesus forgave him less than the woman because Simon probably led a good life and had sins that may not have been as grave as those of the woman. Jesus, however, reveals to him that God looks at things differently: the woman offered Jesus everything she had and was. Her love was absolutely unconditional and her intention to be forgiven was unquestionable. Nothing in the world could have stopped her from coming to Jesus, not even a Pharisee like Simon, who was used to judging people and telling them what to do.

Jesus attacked not the life and actions of Simon, but his convictions and his method of relating to others. In many respects, Simon was no better than the sinful woman. In fact, in certain ways the woman was far better than Simon. Simon did not give Jesus water for His feet but the woman bathed them with her tears and dried them with her hair. It was a custom that men gave each other the kiss of peace in Jesus' society, but Simon somehow overlooked this when welcoming Jesus to dinner. The sinful woman, however, did not stop kissing Jesus' feet from the time she entered Simon's house. Simon did not anoint Jesus' head (a sign of welcome and hospitality), whereas the woman anointed Jesus' feet with ointment.

The parallel between the actions of Simon and the woman is very interesting. Jesus compares Simon who is clinging to the reputation he has in the city with the woman who does not have anything to cling to except Jesus' love and forgiveness. Simon believes what everybody else believes; the woman believes in what Jesus believes. Simon follows rules and regulations that were created by social convictions; the woman follows exclusively the rules of Jesus. Simon is waiting to see what actions Jesus will take; the woman reaches out to Jesus to benefit from His infinite love. Simon wants to categorize Jesus; the woman, although a sinner, seeks forgiveness and approval by Jesus.

As a result of the woman's action, Jesus publicly declares that "her sins, many as they are, have been forgiven, and so she has shown great love" (Lk 7:47). Simon, on the other hand, does not love Jesus like the woman does. The conclusion is, "whoever is forgiven little, loves little" (Lk 7:47).

There is a great joy in the heart of the sinful woman who experienced the forgiveness of the Lord. By word and deed, Jesus released her from a burden that she carried with much pain and shame. Her suffering was obvious because she was crying. She was in contact with herself and was aware of her situation. As sinful as she felt, she did not cast her problem aside. She faced her own situation in a realistic way and approached Jesus for help. Resolutely, at the very end of the scene, Jesus praised her faith: "Your faith has saved you, go in peace" (Lk 7:50).

In many of His healing miracles, Jesus healed people from their physical illness and then uttered words of spiritual healing. When Jesus healed a paralytic or blind person and then stated that their sins were forgiven, they did not have the slightest problem in believing Him. In fact, Jesus' power of physical healing was a guarantee of the spiritual healing (forgiveness of sins) that had taken place.

Jesus did not heal the repentant woman physically. Therefore, His power of forgiving her sins was not demonstrated by any tangible miracle. Why would the woman then believe that her sins were really forgiven? It seems that something powerful was taking place inside her. It is impossible to know what she was experiencing. It is obvious that she had heard about Jesus from others and deliberately came to meet Him. Yet, there is still something that none of us can fully know: the very intimate experience that was taking place in her tormented heart, the experience of her personal faith.

"Your faith has saved you, go in peace" (Lk 7:50) are the final words Jesus uttered in the scene. In a society where everybody turned their backs on her, this woman felt in the very depth of her heart an understanding Lord Who did not judge her. At the root of her initiative to come to Jesus there was an extraordinary faith that the Lord would do something for her. There was something very spiritual, very deep inside of her. An explosion of love, repentance, and faith poured out of her heart.

For the "sinful" woman, a new life had begun. Her faith had saved her. She experienced peace, salvation, and conversion. Apart from the mention that Jesus was dining with some Jewish leaders, the entire focus of the scene shifted to this special encounter between Him and the woman. This encounter would change her life forever. On the outside she was crying; on the inside she was sorry for her sins. Her whole being was moved by meeting the Lord and she was given the grace and the courage to begin a new way of life. Encountering the Lord fulfilled the longings of her anxious heart.

How can the story of this woman be a model for today's women if they persist in the belief that they never sin, that all their acts are good as long as they feel good about them? Is it possible for this Gospel story to show a modern twenty-first century woman that it is a mistake for her to feel she is entitled to have her own private system of moral values? She needs to know that there is a divine law inscribed in the very depth of her conscience and heart. The encounter between Jesus and the sinful woman warns against a false understanding of one's relationship with oneself, God, and the world. The woman in this Gospel realized that her life was not in order, that she needed to do something about that; the temptation for modern women is to feel that a new "reality" allows them to abandon many moral traditions as no longer applicable and, hence, not to do anything to put their life in order.

The sinful woman, in her encounter with Jesus, showed the deep sorrow her conscience was experiencing. Despite repeating the same shameful acts, her conscience somehow remained sensitive about what was good and what was evil. The Gospel according to Luke invites women to resist the temptation of losing the sense of conscience. Because of their Christian upbringing, some women feel guilty when they commit an evil act for the first time. Their parents and the Church have taught them to distinguish between good and evil. They grew up with those convictions, although they started to challenge them when they reached a certain age (high school or college). Repeating the same sins over and over again brings a heavy burden of guilt. They find themselves fragile and distraught. Desperate to find relief from the guilt and shame they feel, they see two options: either they confirm that their actions are wrong and they determine to change them, or they throw out the law of the Lord because they feel nobody can live up to it.

As a result, certain actions, although long considered evil, become accepted by society as natural and normal. Rejecting such twisted norms is a very challenging task for women. In fact, most of the time, they find themselves living in a non-supportive community. Their friends mock them if they hold to "traditional" values and describe those values as "outdated." Although our society claims to be open to others' way of thinking, it is still obvious that certain people's convictions are not respected simply because they are different from the new "reality."

Convinced that the "real" thing is to follow what everybody is doing, many of today's women assume certain positions on current issues and refuse to change their opinion about them. Actions that at first produced a sense of guilt, now become right and acceptable because it is hard to avoid such actions. After all, everybody is doing them. As a result, many contemporary women, as smart and efficient in life as they are, lose their connection with Christian moral principles entirely.

Often they continue making wrong choices because worldly

pressure is so strong. To do whatever everybody else is doing is the easy thing. It takes a lot of courage to go against the flow. Therefore, we ought to respect the painful experiences that all women have had in their emancipation history. The feelings they have about the relationship between their own experience and the Church's teachings are valid considerations, indeed.

Many women have experienced some hard knocks in life and are no longer able to connect with the Church's moral teachings. How can we ask them to be open to ideas and theories that don't mean anything to them anymore? Are we open to understand that some of them are suffering so much that they don't care anymore? Shouldn't we try to support them in their pain even when they feel that God and the Church have abandoned them? The reality is that some women feel that the teaching of Christ and the Church is not realistic at all. When we acknowledge their complaints and try to open a dialogue with them, we learn many wonderful things they themselves learned through suffering. What they have learned from the hardships they have endured is often remarkable. They need time and an understanding community in order to stand tall again. Later they will make a great contribution to the Church based on their knowledge of adversity.

The experience of these women, however, should not be presented as the measure for the truth about God and righteous human life in this world. The only source for such a criterion is God Who has revealed His will to the Church in and through Christ by the power of the Holy Spirit. But God understands the pain women suffer and wants them to be at peace and to renew always their original spark of love for life. Through prayer, dialogue, and, above all, through love, the Church can realize the sincerity and awesome character of their life experience.

In the Gospel of Luke, the encounter between the sinful woman and Christ says something about the experience of today's women. The community of the Church appreciates and respects the sufferings they have had in the past. However, Christ invites them to incorporate their own sufferings with His and reach beyond it. Women are called to experience the fullness of life that Christ gives to every human person through His death and Resurrection. If they consider the past as a learning experience and seek the truth in it, they will find it and thus fulfill the longing in their hearts.

Nothing prevented the woman of the Gospel from coming to Jesus and weeping at His feet. She did not ignore the evil character of her past deeds. Rather, she recognized with repentant heart, the seriousness of her sins and the void they left in her life. Recognizing the evil of sin became the first step to correct her life. The fact that she repeatedly committed the same sins over and over again did not keep her heavy conscience from recognizing the evil of her sins. Only Jesus was able to restore peace and dignity to a life that was tarnished by the seriousness of her sins and miserable circumstances. Although she never lost her dignity entirely since she was created in God's image, she well knew that not all her actions were good. She recognized that some were truly evil and degrading. But, at the same time, she realized that her past did not determine her future in an absolute sense. Recognizing evil and sin was the first step, repenting and resolving to do good came about when she was freed by Christ.

Contrary to Gospel values and under the excuse of a mistaken impression of dignity, many women have a very hard time recognizing evil at work in their lives. If all human actions are acceptable as "normal" and "natural," there would be no evil, a fact that contradicts both divine revelation and our daily experience. A true peace cannot be earned, unless everyone turns to Jesus, recognizes the evil they have done and accepts from Jesus, with humility, forgiveness for their sins.

Ultimately, it all comes down to the same point: Do we believe that God has established the standard for what is good and what is evil? Or do humans decide for themselves what is good and what is evil? This is the most tormenting dilemma that contemporary people face in their relationship with God: Why do God and the Church consider evil what they have convinced themselves is good? The struggle between the human mind and will and the Divine Mind and Will began with Adam and Eve and continues to this day!

Generous Women Support Jesus Financially
(Luke 8:1-3)

It happened next that he went travelling through city and village, preaching and proclaiming the good news of the Kingdom of God, and the Twelve were with him as well as some women who had been healed from evil spirits and illnesses — Mary, who was called the Magdalene, from whom seven demons had gone out, and Joanna, the wife of Chuza, Herod's steward, and Susanna, and many others who provided for them out of their possessions.[8]

This short report of Saint Luke about Jesus' activity relates several historical facts surrounding Jesus' life. Jesus did not travel alone when He went about preaching God's kingdom in the towns and villages of Palestine. With Him were a number of disciples (among them twelve whom He would designate as His Apostles) and a group of women. These constituted a kind of "inner circle" around Jesus who were privy to more details than others about His person and His plan of redemption.

What interests us here especially is the group of women who were following Jesus. They were Mary Magdalene, Joanna, Susanna, and a number of others who provided for Jesus and the Apostles "out of their possessions." Who are these women and why were they associated with the Lord? How were they able to provide for Jesus and the Apostles "out of their possessions"? What are the implications of their generosity on Jesus' activity?

Was it just money that constituted their possessions? Or could "possessions" also include domestic chores like cooking, cleaning, doing the laundry? Undoubtedly these women did not only support Him financially. They must also have played a domestic role in their service of Jesus and His disciples.

Mary Magdalene is described as a healed person out of whom seven demons had been driven. The number seven in the Bible signifies in this case the maximum number possible, and indicates something of the depth of her troubles before encountering the Lord. Jesus, according to all four Gospels, completely changed her life and she became a disciple who followed Him everywhere He went. Later, she became an apostle to the Apostles in announcing to them the Resurrection of Jesus from the dead.

Joanna was the wife of king Herod's steward, Chuza. This implies that she was a wealthy woman because her husband held an eminent position in the palace of the king. We do not know how she managed to be close to Jesus or why she ended up following Him in His ministry. It is obvious that the Lord had somehow changed her life so profoundly that she wanted to repay Him in the best way she felt she could. It may be that she was introduced to Jesus through other women who were familiar with His activity and life. In any case, a woman in her position could spend a lot of money on the daily things Jesus and the Twelve needed to sustain them in their work.

We know less about Susanna and the many other women who provided for Jesus and the Twelve out of their resources. What impressed Luke about these women was not so much who they were but how generous they were in assisting the Lord and the Twelve. Without their generosity it would not have been possible for Jesus and His disciples to dedicate themselves to preaching the Good News the way they did. Even though they could count on the legendary hospitality of the people of that region, there were limits. It is difficult to assume that Jesus and His followers could eat everyday without having some kind of regular support upon which they could depend.

While all the ways in which these Galilean women supported Jesus and His disciples is not clear, there is no question that their role was not limited to providing money for their expenses. If they accompanied Jesus and the Twelve, they undoubtedly also involved themselves in spreading the Good News. However, they did so in their own way and according to the methods women in general employed to influence others in their society. They were more readily able to introduce other women to Jesus and facilitate their conversion. Joanna, Mary Magdalene, and Susanna had much easier access to other women than Jesus and the disciples. Although thousands of men and women followed Jesus and listened to His teaching, women such as Mary Magdalene and her friends were able to follow up on Jesus' activity and to preach in their own way to other women.

From this account we are again witnesses to issues that break the rules established by the society of the time. We see females publicly involved with male leaders, we see male leaders accepting female involvement and further yet, we see females asserting the role of providers that was definitely not typical in Jesus' time. As many women in the history of the Church have done before them, today's women should take stock of what these early Galilean women did to promote salvation through Christ. Whether financially or by other supportive means such as missionary work, involvement with humanitarian efforts, volunteering at their local parish, or simply reaching out to help others on an individual basis, women can act as the Lord's messengers and vehicles in accomplishing the grace of God both here and now, today, and in paving the way for others to carry on their work.

Jesus Praises the Faith of Two Sisters
(Luke 10:38-42)

In the course of their journey he entered a certain village where a woman named Martha received him. She
had a sister named Mary who seated herself at the Lord's
feet and listened to his teaching. But Martha was dis-
tracted with all the serving, so she came up and said,
"Lord, doesn't it matter to you that my sister has left
me to serve alone? Tell her to give me a hand!" In response the Lord said to her, "Martha, Martha! You're
anxious and upset over many things, but one thing is
necessary. Mary has chosen the better part, which will
not be taken from her."[9]

Martha and Mary (this Mary is not Mary the Mother of Jesus)
were the sisters of Lazarus, whom Jesus raised from the dead. Lazarus and his two sisters were close friends of Jesus. They opened
their home to the Lord and invited Him often to eat with them.
They lived in a village called Bethany, near Jerusalem.

The Evangelist Luke reports that on one of His journeys Jesus
entered the house of Mary, Martha and Lazarus. According to
Middle-Eastern customs, a guest is normally welcomed at the door
of the house. If the guest is an important person, the people of the
house even go outside the house to receive the guest with signs of
respect and reverence. It seems that Martha happened to be the
one who "welcomed Jesus" at the door when He came to visit.

Luke begins to describe the activity of Mary, Martha's sister,
who "seated herself at the Lord's feet and listened to his teaching."
It was a custom in Jesus' time for teachers to have followers wherever they went. They formed a kind of circle of disciples who listened to the teacher's instructions and then applied them. In Scripture, we see Jesus delivering speeches to a variety of audiences, on
many occasions, and in many different places. He goes up the

mountain and preaches a sermon on the Beatitudes. He sits on the boat and teaches the crowd on shore. He stands in the fields to instruct His listeners about the meaning of the bread of life, the Eucharist. He stops in the middle of a crowded road to heal the blind and to teach about the kingdom of God. Jesus was and is the Divine Teacher responsible for spreading the Good News of the kingdom of God.

Jesus did not always instruct great numbers of people. In many instances, He was just surrounded by a small circle of disciples. These were, on occasion, the twelve Apostles and some women who were His closest friends and supporters. These small sessions were more intimate because Jesus addressed this "inner circle" of His followers in a more special way. Their love and appreciation of the Lord was often represented in physical contact. Hence we see John the Evangelist leaning on Jesus' chest during the Last Supper, asking who would betray Him. The "sinful" woman cried at the feet of Jesus wiping them with her hair. The man delivered from the possession of a demon sits at the feet of Jesus (Lk 8:35). Mary Magdalene clung to the feet of Jesus after His Resurrection listening to His word. Jesus Himself invited the Apostles to touch His hands and His feet after His Resurrection in order to be confirmed in their faith. Even Saint Paul, a Jew, born in Tarsus in Cilicia, but brought up in Jerusalem, himself confesses, "At the feet of Gamaliel, I was educated strictly, according to the Torah we received from our ancestors, and was zealous for God, just as all of you are today" (Ac 22:3).

Being at the feet of Jesus listening to His word is a very humble position. Mary acknowledges the sovereignty of Jesus and the authority of His teaching. John the Baptist has already said that he is not worthy to untie the sandal strap of Jesus (Jn 1:27) indicating the superiority of Christ. By sitting at the feet of Jesus, Mary's gesture expresses her submission to Jesus' truthfulness and authority. Through her bodily gesture she expressed her desire to be totally open to the Lord's teachings.

At the time of Jesus, it was customary for men to sit at the feet of the teacher to receive instruction. So it is remarkable in first-century Palestinian Judaism that a woman should assume the posture of a disciple at the master's feet.[10] This fact reveals a characteristic attitude of Jesus toward women especially in Luke's Gospel. Jesus directly involves women in the plan of salvation and, as the Teacher of the New Law, instructs them concerning the kingdom of God.

Saint Luke also describes the activity of Martha who, burdened with much serving, was complaining about her sister Mary: "Lord, doesn't it matter to you that my sister has left me to serve alone? Tell her to give me a hand." Receiving important guests such as Jesus and His disciples requires a lot of work. Martha was obviously preparing a good meal and needed the help of Mary. Her complaint is quite valid because sisters are supposed to help each other in such situations. A woman who neglected to help her mother or her sister on an occasion like this would be labeled as lazy and, therefore, could lose the respect of her community.

Jesus' response to Martha conveys the real purpose of the entire story: "Martha, Martha! You're anxious and upset over many things, but one thing is necessary. Mary has chosen the better part, which will not be taken from her" (Lk 10:41-42). Whereas most people would agree that Mary should be helping Martha in serving, Jesus sees the situation from a different angle. He challenges the conventional opinion and praises Mary's desire to dedicate her time to listening to what He had to say. We assume that Mary was also good at serving, but given the opportunity she chose to listen and to learn from the greatest teacher of all time, Jesus, the Divine Master.

First of all, Jesus is not comparing something good to something bad. Rather, He compares something good with something "better." There is no question that working around the house and preparing food for guests is a good thing. Hospitality and generosity are qualities praised by Scriptures. They reflect God's perfect generosity toward humanity. Without the work of Martha, Jesus would not have been fed that day.

Nowhere in the Gospel does Jesus ignore or undermine the importance of life's duties. They are part of human existence and we must all take care of them. Human needs should never be considered as an insignificant dimension of our lives because God has established them as a means of our sanctification. Jesus was not criticizing Martha; rather, He was pointing out that she allowed her worldly duties to take on an importance they did not have. Instead of inviting her to stop doing her job, He suggested a better way to approach things. Worry and anxiety about things is not the answer.

Jesus invites Martha to look at all things and to understand them in and through the light of God. God gives us the wisdom to deal with worldly affairs. This wisdom conditions our relation to the world and shapes it. The word of God enables us to look at the world and understand it the way God wants us to. Although working in the world with the intention of making it a better place for God's kingdom is important, God's word and His will are always more important. In this sense, Mary has chosen the better part, whereas Martha — whose priorities were fixed on this world — has allowed her work to fill her with worry and anxiety.

In the story of Martha and Mary, Jesus presents the relationship between God's word and human work. Jesus establishes the essence of that relationship: it is better to listen to God's word than to do anything else in this world. This role will never be taken from Mary. Who can deprive her of the privilege of listening to Jesus' word and enjoying it? On many occasions we could be deprived of certain work we want to do, even if it is a good work. However, we should never be deprived of the possibility to listen to what Jesus has to say to us. His word provides the ultimate framework for every single activity we do in our lives.

Notice that Jesus did not say that Mary's part alone is enough. He said it is a "better part." Mary still needs to do some work and help her sister. On the one hand, Jesus accepts the work of Martha and invites her not to worry. On the other hand, Jesus praises Mary's listening to His word while not excluding the possibility of her work. Thus, in the story of Martha and Mary Jesus recommends a balance between human work and listening to God's word.

Nobody does anything, even an evil action, without thinking that they are doing what is ultimately right and good for them. So when Martha is convinced that it is wrong to be like Mary, it is hard to open a discussion with her. Reintroducing Jesus and His teaching becomes an almost impossible task.

The only way Christ can play an active role in the life of today's working woman is for her to have an experience that reconnects Christ with her world. But can anyone help her to have such an experience? The answer is yes. We, as Church and God's people, cannot experience Christ for her or instead of her, but we can facilitate the way to her own experience. No matter how modern, rich, or up-to-date she is, she is still a creature of God endowed with love and natural goodness. Every woman, just because she is a woman, has goodness inscribed in her very nature and, therefore, has a basic experience of God. With this in mind, can we not determine how faith in Jesus' way to eternal salvation can be restored in their lives? They must sit like Mary at His feet and listen.

Jesus often ran into women who were spending their entire life frustrated about many things. In the same way today, women suffer endlessly from mundane matters instead of meditating on the mystery of their human existence. Yet, the answer is right there around the corner of their hearts. Being busy with work, family life, and having fun, are all good things; however, they become empty promises if a woman's hopes hang on those things alone.

The good news of our salvation in Christ gives real and lasting meaning to life. If everything they do is seen in the light of eternity, women can enjoy life on earth and live in relative comfort. This way of relating to their life experiences is the key to their ultimate success. Christ invites them to look at things with His eyes and through His mind. Life becomes so much easier when they deal with things according to God's logic rather than through their mere human perceptions.

How can they do that? The answer is simple: use this world as if it is not being used. Enjoy all of creation, yet leave room for what is eternal. Enjoy the opportunities life offers and yet remember that what you do should be directed to an endless sharing in God's life. Look through one eye at the things of the earth and through the other eye at God's mystery. This balance constitutes the ultimate challenge to women who, as faithful as they are to Christ, are daily immersed in the many worries and concerns of life. The key is to be both Martha and Mary.

The other model the Evangelist Luke gives is Mary who sat at the feet of Jesus listening to His words. If Mary chose to meditate at the feet of Jesus, it does not mean that she did not work at all. At that moment, however, she dedicated her entire attention to the Word of God. Jesus praised her for this, saying that she had chosen the better part. In fact, throughout the Gospels, Jesus considers the business of His Father above every other work that a human being can perform.

Jesus' special appreciation of Mary's choice constitutes a model for all women following in the footsteps of the Lord. No matter how much good work a woman can do in life, it will be impossible for her to develop an authentic spirituality without taking time for prayer, meditation and listening to God's word. Jesus Himself was reported to have spent entire nights in communion with His Father. Although He constantly worked to proclaim the kingdom of God, Jesus made it a point to put everything aside each day and dedicate a time to prayer in communion with the Father. Jesus' example reveals that, by God's standard, prayer is essential. It expresses the absolute and total dependence of human beings on God.

To listen to God's word, to meditate, and to pray, are very hard things to do in this hyperactive world. Modern women cannot easily relate to these quiet times anymore. The last thing a woman wants to do is to be like Mary sitting still at the feet of Jesus listening to His word when there is so much that needs to be done. A contemporary woman would rather do something or talk about something than to sit and do nothing. She is afraid to be silent and to listen. Why?

The example of Mary at the feet of Jesus invites contemporary woman to be comfortable with thinking about life and her place in the scheme of things. Jesus' praise of Mary's attitude is directed to every woman who is not afraid of facing herself. Jesus invites every woman to discover and know herself in silence. Listening to the Lord speaking in the depths of her heart enables a woman to know who she truly is.

A series of painful experiences may bring a woman to have low self-esteem. Recent studies show that a high percentage of women do not like themselves, although they are wonderful human beings. They often try to cover their pain with laughter, a busy life, and many friendships. Perhaps they fear that, if they are quiet and listen, they may discover something more that they don't like about themselves. How can they fully appreciate themselves when others have disparaged them for so many years? Jesus understands, as in the case of Mary, the need of those women to listen to His comforting words.

Here is the challenge: How can we convince today's woman that she is essentially a good person? How can we convince her that God loves her simply because she is an individual created in His own image and likeness? Is it possible to make her believe that it is wonderful for her to be herself and that God cares about that? As in the example of Mary, can we present meditation and listening in silence as positive things that will help her discover her true identity?

The example of Mary in the Gospel provides fundamental support for every woman who embarks on the long journey of self-discovery. Jesus considers Mary's ability to listen to God's word a praiseworthy and necessary thing. Mary invites others to take that first step towards meditation, which is normally the most difficult one. Just sit at the feet of the Lord and listen. It takes a lot of humility and openness to set everything aside and listen to Jesus speaking. Once a woman starts this long journey, she will realize what a wonderful creature she is. She has always been such, but she needs to experience it for herself.

If a woman wants to recognize her true identity, dignity, and vocation, she has only to listen to Jesus. This is beautifully stated by the Second Vatican Council: "It is only in the light of the Word made flesh that the mystery of man and woman is revealed" (GS, 22). Christ, and only Christ, can make a woman appreciate the mystery of her own existence. Listening to Jesus' word is the first step on the journey of understanding that mystery.

Our world today needs a balance between work and prayer, between doing and listening to God's word. This eternal word is often drowned out by the voices of the world. Jesus believes in every woman's capacity to listen to Him. The Lord speaks to the heart in every occasion. If everyone would listen, as Mary did, miracles would happen in their lives. Every woman needs to discover herself and God's word in her life. If there were another way than listening to Jesus, He would have never failed to show it to the humanity He redeemed with His blood. Jesus says: "I am the Way, the Truth, and the Life."

Every Woman Is a Daughter of Abraham
(Luke 13:10-17)

> Now he was teaching in one of the synagogues on the Sabbath. And, behold, a woman was there who for eighteen years had had a crippling spirit, and she was bent over double and unable to straighten herself up fully. When Jesus saw her he called out to her and said, "Woman, you've been set free from your illness!" Then

he laid his hands on her and she straightened up immediately and began glorifying God. The ruler of the synagogue was indignant that Jesus had healed on the Sabbath, so in response he said to the crowd, "There are
six days on which it is proper to perform work, so come
be healed on those days and not on the Sabbath!" But
the Lord answered him and said, "You hypocrites! Don't
each of you untie your ox or donkey from the manger
and lead it off to water on the Sabbath? Wasn't it proper
for this daughter of Abraham, whom Satan had bound
for all these eighteen years, to be released from this bond
on the Sabbath day?" And when he said these things all
his opponents were put to shame, and the whole crowd
rejoiced at all the glorious things that were done by him.[11]

According to Jewish custom, when a Jewish visitor attended
the service at the synagogue on Saturday (Sabbath), he was often
invited to speak or present some kind of a teaching. This text tells
us that Jesus was in the synagogue "teaching" on a Sabbath when
He noticed the presence of an woman who was ill. He healed her
despite the controversy that He knew His action would cause.

This woman was crippled for eighteen years and was unable
to stand erect. Obviously, everybody knew her in the village and
was aware that it was impossible for her to recover her full health.
People were used to seeing her every day in that situation and probably had lost hope for any possible cure. Her presence in the synagogue attracted attention because everyone knew of the power of
Jesus and the miracles He had been performing. People were watching to see what Jesus would do; the sick woman was also observ-
ing Jesus and anxiously anticipating His next move; Jesus, in turn,
was watching both her and the people. The tension in the synagogue was palpable. Observers, including the women, were half expecting a miracle, and Jesus immediately saw a situation in which
He could demonstrate the converting power of faith.

The woman did not ask for a miracle. Jesus took the initiative and said: "Woman, you've been set free from your illness." He laid His hands on her and at once she stood up straight and glorified God. There is no way for us to know why Jesus chose this specific woman to heal. He usually tested the will of the sick person to see if he or she believed. In this instance, Jesus acted immediately without seeking any proof that the woman believed in Him. This shows the supreme authority of the Lord Who chooses the kind of action He thinks will most benefit humanity. It also indicates that Jesus' initiative can be understood only in the light of God's standards. God alone knew what the effects of Jesus' intervention in the life of this woman would be and what kind of conversion His healing power would bring about in her.

The context in which the miracle took place is not friendly to Jesus because surrounding Him were Jewish officials who considered the Sabbath a day of rest on which such work was prohibited. Therefore, the Jewish leader was "indignant" because Jesus showed no respect for the Law. But was it because the healing took place on the Sabbath, or was it also because the people were impressed with Jesus' performance, a fact that provoked jealousy in the synagogue leader? Was a miracle really considered "work" according to Jewish Law?

Jesus does not leave the audience without explaining His reasons for the miracle. He argues from the lesser to the greater: If you loose animals on the Sabbath, why not loose a human from her disabilities on the Sabbath? If Jewish Law does not object to having animals be loosed on the Sabbath, why would the same Law object to freeing people from the bondage of sin? Aren't human beings more important than animals? Wasn't the Jewish Law made for people and not people for the Law?

The fact that a simple woman was "glorifying God" in front of everyone there provoked the anger of the synagogue leader. Women did not play any role during a Jewish service on the Sabbath. Organizing and leading prayers was the job of men. Jesus,

Who was not the leader of that synagogue, was viewed as intruding on the leader's authority by performing a miracle and allowing a woman to publicly praise God: "This 'little one' (the woman) who responds to God's kingdom power in her life by praising God, is contrasted with the religious leader, whose views of when God can act blind him to the presence of that kingdom and his need for repentance."[12]

It is obvious that the leader of the synagogue resents Jesus' popularity. Jesus had already acquired a positive reputation by performing miracles that none of the Jewish leaders were able to do or to refute. Another public miracle simply added more wonderment in the hearts of the people who were already very impressed with Jesus.

When God created heaven and earth, the Bible relates that God rested on the Sabbath (Saturday), the seventh day. With the call of Abraham, the nation of Israel was brought into existence. God established a covenant with Abraham, making him the father of many nations. One essential component of this covenant was the consecration of the seventh day, the Sabbath, to God. Every Jew was invited to abstain from work and toil on the Sabbath because it was a holy day of rest. Jews go to the synagogue, the Jewish prayer place, in order to read Scriptures and pray the psalms.

Why was meeting publicly and healing an ill woman on the Sabbath such a challenging moment in Jesus' ministry among the Jews? After all, it all took place in the synagogue, in the presence of Jewish leaders. Jesus goes out of His way to identify this sick woman as a daughter of Abraham, the common father of them all in the faith and the founder of Israel. He was and is a model for every Jew who belongs to the people of the Old Covenant. Jews considered it a matter of great pride to be part of the chosen people because God had promised to bestow His special blessings on them. For many pious Jews, this religious heritage meant more to them than to have a close personal relationship with God. Males were consecrated to God as inheritors of the covenant through the rite of circumcision. They, therefore, often felt that they had a right to certain blessings and privileges denied to women. But this line of thinking does not hold water with Jesus because He sees it as a misinterpretation of Scripture. Being a child of Abraham is not restricted to the healthy or to males. The sick woman should also receive the blessing of Abraham because she belongs to the new and reconstituted Israel, the Church.

What does this mean for us? According to Saint Luke, the people of the New Covenant are the new chosen people of God, the Church. The Old Covenant has been replaced. This Church is the beginning, the seed, of the kingdom of God. All people of all races and nationalities are invited to belong to this kingdom. Members of both sexes share equally in its promises. The sick, the blind, the poor, and the weak are all welcome. Signs of the presence of God's kingdom include the destruction of sin and evil. The Lord interacts with the sick woman, heals her, and manifests the effects of God's kingdom on her life. Jesus delivered her from evil: what He has done for her is in fulfillment of His commission to release the captives from their bonds.

By healing this woman on the Sabbath Jesus clarifies the ultimate purpose behind God's holy day; the Sabbath is a celebration of release from the fallen condition of the human race. Its purpose is fulfilled not by forbidding works of compassion, but by encouraging them. No human being has authority to change the deep significance of this day as God intended it when He first established His Covenant with Israel and then with all of humanity in and through Jesus Christ. If the law, as interpreted by Jewish tradition, allowed for the untying of bound animals on the Sabbath, how much more should this woman who had been bound by Satan's power be freed on the Sabbath from her affliction!

It is obvious that today we focus more on God's love, goodness, and mercy. Yet, we should never fail to be aware of the presence and work of evil in our world. Indeed, the conviction of such a presence is found throughout the Scriptures. Jesus directly refers in this passage to Satan who "had bound [the woman] for all these eighteen years" (Lk 13:16). He connects her infirmity with the work and power of Satan. Therefore, the physical healing Jesus bestowed on her also indicates a spiritual deliverance from the power of evil.

In Scripture, however, sin and evil are not necessarily linked to physical illness. In fact, the example of Job illustrates that, despite the fact that God allowed Job to be tested by physical illness and by the loss of his family, God praised the righteousness of Job against the evil acts of his enemies. Jesus Himself clarifies in John 9 that it was not the fault of the blind man that he was blind. Nor was it the fault of his parents. The only reason for his blindness was that God's mysterious mercy might be shown.

In the case of the sick woman, it seems that her physical illness may have been directly related to the power of Satan. Affliction and infirmity are taken as evidence of Satan's hold on humanity. However, the healing ministry of Jesus reveals the gradual wresting away from Satan of his control over humanity and the establishment of God's kingdom.

Jesus came to bring to light the work of God, His Father. Therefore, He sets this woman free and, at the same time, reveals the true meaning of the Sabbath. Namely, that God cares about the human person as such, beyond all laws and rules. If freeing people from sin and evil is the ultimate purpose of the Sabbath, then Jesus does not contradict the Sabbath when He frees people from evil on that day!

Jesus' logic impressed all those present. It triggered two reactions: His adversaries are humiliated and the whole crowd rejoices at the splendid deed done by Him. How is it possible that simple people would be on Jesus' side against their own leaders? Every devout Jew took very seriously the authority and the power of Jewish religious leaders. However, actions speak louder than words: Jesus was doing everything right; His healing generates salvation, gratefulness, peace, and joy.

The fact that the sick woman was physically crippled also describes also her moral situation. The burden of life and sin, the limitations of her human condition, all contribute to making her crippled. The God-man Jesus Christ, God in flesh, meets her and infuses into her His divine energy. Where Jesus is, there is life and healing. God's human face looks into this woman's face and shows her what it means to be part of His kingdom here on earth. The tragic part of this story, however, is the reaction of His enemies. They do not want this sick woman to be completely healed of a long-term illness because they still represent, not God, but the power of evil in the world.

The enemies of Jesus still abound in our world today. Even in the name of religion or religious practices, many become upset when the good Lord intervenes in the lives of so many women to heal them. Whether it is jealousy or hatred, the attitude of Jesus' enemies is still the expression of evil's power in our world. It takes a lot of humility and understanding to accept the fact that God intervenes in some lives when we judge them unworthy of His divine support. How easy it is to judge others and presume to establish the criteria of God's action in others' lives!

The Cry of the Persistent Widow
(Luke 18:1-8)

Then he told them a parable about the need for them to pray always and not become discouraged, saying, "There was a judge in a certain city who neither feared God nor felt shame before men. Now there was a widow in that city who kept coming to him and saying, 'Do me justice against my adversary!' For a while he didn't want to, but later he said to himself, 'Even though I neither fear God nor feel shame, still, because of the way this widow keeps bothering me, I'll do her justice so she won't keep coming and finally wear me out.'" Then the Lord

said, "Listen to what the unjust judge says! Won't God,
then, vindicate His chosen ones when they cry out to
Him day and night and be patient with them? I tell you,
He'll do them justice with all speed. But, nevertheless,
when the Son of Man comes, will he find faith on
earth?"[13]

Two major Gospel themes are expressed in this parable: the
coming of the Son of Man and the power of prayer. God will never
abandon the elect because Jesus will come again to judge all people;
believers must remain faithful and be people of steadfast prayer until
He comes. The faithfulness of God is embodied by the presence of
Jesus Christ in history. His presence inaugurates the kingdom of
God, a kingdom that will last forever. Therefore, God's faithfulness
is a given fact experienced through the tangible presence of Jesus
Christ.

In the Gospel according to Luke, especially in this parable,
prayer is not merely a communication with God. It is the result of
fidelity to God in all circumstances of life. Fidelity and prayer are
mutually related: fidelity must be the engine of prayer; prayer
strengthens the person's fidelity to God. In order to be faithful, one
must pray. In turn, prayer is motivated by the desire to be faithful.

The widow was begging the judge to render a just decision
for her against her adversaries. What she was asking for is nothing
but justice. She could not understand why the unjust judge wouldn't
help her case. If she had the right to win the situation, was she ignored because she was a widow? The fact that the unjust judge did
not fear God and did not respect any human being describes him
clearly: he was both ruthless and arrogant. He wouldn't even help
a poor widow who most certainly had a notoriously hard life in those
days. Such a woman, deprived of her male protector in a patriar-
chal society, is the picture of total powerlessness.

While thinking about the widow's case, the unjust judge con-
cluded that he would help her because he didn't want her to strike

him. The term "strike" suggests the extreme situation to which the persistence of the widow might lead. It could also indicate that she would "wear him out" if he didn't help her. Perhaps, she also has a "connection" with some rough men who could help her get her revenge against the unjust judge. In a word, the weak widow's persistence was the threat to the powerful judge.

The only reason that made the judge answer the widow's request was her persistence and his fear of the possible consequences. He did not care about justice. He forgot that, as a judge, he was supposed to reflect God's impartiality in rendering justice. Although he dealt with worldly relationships between people, he was still endowed with that authority by God. In this case, he was abusing authority given to him by God Himself. He misunderstood his position of power as a personal privilege which led him to his unjust and arrogant attitude.

Jesus draws a parallel between God's function as a judge and the unjust judge. Two lessons are drawn from the argument of the helpless widow: (1) If the persistent pleading of the helpless widow triumphs over an unjust judge, how much more will the persistent praying of Christian disciples achieve? (2) If an unjust judge yields to the entreaties of a widow, how much more will a just and gracious God grant to a woman who prays to Him with persistence?

The main purpose of this parable is to show the power that the Christians have in persistent and humble prayer. The insistence of the weakest person, the widow, results in possession of God's power. With this parable the first Christians realized how God functions: God wants Jesus' disciple to depend absolutely on Him through persistent pleading. The infinite distance between the unjust judge and the graciousness of God makes the effects of faithful prayer even more relevant. It is so much more powerful when God answers the prayer of the weak person than an unjust judge forced to yield to a weak one's insistence. As far as God is concerned, He will see to it that justice is done for every persistent person, no matter how powerless.

In 80 A.D., the community to which Saint Luke is addressing his parable was probably being persecuted. The Evangelist's message is clear: the decisive question is not about God's vindication of His persecuted community, though God will ultimately vindicate them. The decisive question is whether Jesus' disciples will remain faithful to Him during the undetermined length of time before His return.

The contrast between the powerful judge and the weak widow follows a pattern throughout the Gospel of Saint Luke. It highlights the tension between the strength of this world's rulers and the true strength of God's power when connected with weak people. While the unjust judge seems to be in control of the situation, the poor widow is really the one who controls it. In fact, the judge ended up granting her desires. By doing that Luke suggests what God would have done for her in the first place. She had to fight for it, even though it was a right she deserved.

Luke often draws a parallel between the action of the heavenly Father and the action of the human person. The Father's work is far more transcendent and perfect than anything done by a human being. If Jesus nevertheless compares the attitude of the unjust judge to that of God, he does so with the sole intention of emphasizing that even so-called evil people are able to do good. The unjust judge ultimately did the right thing, although he had to be pressured by the widow. Jesus does not criticize the final action of the unjust judge; He criticizes the process of his thinking and the reason behind his action. God, however, will see to it that justice is done for His children simply because they are His chosen ones. Herein lies God's unconditional graciousness in intervening in the life of every one of His children under duress.

This text is critical in the history of the Church because it demonstrates the oft-repeated terrible contrast between power and true power. Down through the centuries there have been many women who have experienced exactly what the poor widow of the Gospel went through with the unjust judge. Often misjudged by authorities, they were ultimately vindicated by the unseen and just judgment of God. It is amazing that suffering injustice has always been part of the Cross that many Saints carried as they preached and lived the teachings of Jesus Christ.

In action, as well as in word, those in power over society have not always treated women justly. Sometimes even when these women lived in a saintly way, they were falsely accused of bad things they did not commit. Nobody listened to them as they were relating what truly happened in their lives. Yet, God has vindicated every single one of them because His justice can never be frustrated by any human system. Many saintly women in history fully embraced the teachings of the Holy Catholic Church. Such faith did not stop authorities from accusing them of heresies. The truth was ultimately manifested to the world, sometimes at the end of their lives or often with their death or afterwards.

Through the centuries, how many women have lived an unseen life of holiness, praying day and night for the world! They were united to Christ throughout their days and considered their life with Him as the most precious of all treasures. Forgotten by the world and society, they lived under the pressure of injustice and nevertheless succeeded in conquering tyranny. In churches all over the world, to this day, women live their mission of preaching Christ, sometimes without saying a word. Despite the sophisticated society in which they exist, their simple hearts reflect the original beauty and simplicity that God intended for the human person from the beginning. Far from being against technology, they use every modern means to praise the wisdom of the Creator Who rules the universe and orders all things for the salvation of humankind.

Every day there is a tension between the weak woman and the powerful and unjust judge. Yet, every day God listens to the cry of the poor and vindicates them. Nothing escapes the knowledge and the power of God. Nothing will ever change His attitude towards those oppressed by human systems. Unfortunately, systems that are created by God to protect and rule human societies with justice are often abused by those who misunderstand the true meaning of "being in power."

Today, people, families, communities, societies and nations are called to realize that God is the sole source of all true power. It is a biblical teaching that every authority is a gift from God and a reflection of God's concern and love for the world and every human person in it. Therefore, the only way to obtain peace is to exercise justice. Based on Scriptures, the relationship between justice and peace is a foremost theme of the social teaching of the Catholic Church since the Second Vatican Council (1962-1965). Realizing the complexity of the social and political situation of today's world, Pope John XXIII, Paul VI, and John Paul II, all encourage the leaders of the world to exercise their power with justice. These smart and "modern" Popes know that there can never be peace in the hearts of people and in the world unless everyone works together to create a just society.

Conclusion:
Promise, Hope, and Surprise

The Gospel according to Saint Luke promises God's assistance to every human person, especially to women, to outcasts, and to the weak. I do not intend to identify women as the weak part of the society, although in Jesus' time they were surely oppressed and lived a very unappreciated life. For Luke, however, despite the failure of the world to respect women's identity and role in life, Jesus presents the ultimate victory of God's logic and work. God wants every woman to experience the fullness of life and salvation.

Whereas human promises are constantly unfulfilled, God's promise assumes a different dimension. What makes God essentially different than all human beings is His being Truth itself. As such, God never tires of assuring every woman that being faithful in their response to Him is what brings them to God's salvation.

The essential promise God made to humanity at the dawn of creation is salvation. Therefore, God reaches to the deepest recesses of every woman's heart and, in a way only known to Him, He gives hope in life and in the purpose of human existence. His promise of salvation is firm.

Reading Luke inspires every woman to realize that there is a reason for hope: although still discriminated against even in today's so-called "advanced" societies, women continue to occupy the center of God's attention. In the most mysterious way, Jesus reveals in the Gospel according to Luke that God notices the feeling and life of every woman. Not even the smallest motion of her heart's desire will pass unnoticed in God's eyes! The consequences of this hope are an inner peace that women experience as they discover how much they are appreciated by Jesus.

Since God's standards rise above human logic, Jesus never fails to surprise the world with God's unconditional love for women. The element of surprise reminds every woman and every person that God cannot be limited by the strictures of human life. God always remains the totally different One. Just when someone thinks that he or she has figured out how God functions, God intervenes and reveals a dimension of life that nobody has dreamed of before.

Notes

[1] See Robert J. Karris, "The Gospel According to Luke," in *The New Jerome Biblical Commentary,* New Jersey: Prentice Hall, 1990, 676.

[2] I have thoroughly studied the theme of Mary in my previous books, *Mary's Pope: John Paul II, Mary, and the Church Since Vatican II* (WI: Sheed and Ward, 2000) and *The Faith of Mary* (New York: Alba House, 2002).

[3] Lk 1:41-45.

[4] One should not confuse this Anna with Saint Anna, the Mother of Mary (Jesus' Mother).

[5] Lk 2:36-38.

[6] Lk 7:11-17.

[7] Ibid.

[8] Lk 8:1-3.

[9] Lk 10:38-42.

[10] Parallel verses about a disciple sitting at the feet of the Master are found in Lk 8:35 and Acts 22:3.

[11] Lk 13:10-17.

[12] Robert J. Karris, The Gospel according to Luke," in *The New Jerome Biblical Commentary,* New Jersey: Prentice Hall, 1990, 705.

[13] Lk 18:1-8.

CHAPTER THREE

The Deeper Insight of Saint John's Theology:
Every Woman Is a Wonderful New Creature in Christ

Introduction

The Gospel according to Saint John differs a great deal from Mark, Luke, and Matthew (these three Evangelists are called Synoptics because they are so similar in content and frequently in style). It does not focus on the kingdom of God through proverbs and parables. Instead, Jesus speaks in long discourses that often refer to His relationship with the heavenly Father. John presents Jesus' ministry as primarily taking place in Jerusalem where, for three years, the Lord enters into controversy against the Jews.

John agrees with Mark, Luke, and Matthew that Jesus often healed persons miraculously. These miracles provide the occasion for deeper insight into Jesus' identity. They reveal the face of God in Jesus and thus God's involvement in the very history of the world. Every encounter between Jesus and His people contributes more to the discovery of Who Jesus is.[1]

John is perfectly clear in his Gospel regarding the identity of Jesus. Jesus is the Son of God, the very Word of God made flesh. He was in the beginning with God the Father. From all eternity, even before the world existed, Jesus was present with the Father and the Holy Spirit. All that exists came to be through Him. On one occasion Jesus stated very clearly that He and the Father are one (Jn 10:30). More than the other three Evangelists, John emphatically insists on the divinity of Christ.

The fact that Christ is divine explains why His work and mission were able to be effective. He came to repair the breach caused by the offense occasioned by our first parents against divine justice. Because an infinite God was offended reparation would have to be infinite as well. Christ alone, God and man, could make amends and bring salvation to the whole human race. Jesus is a God of salvation: He is the source of eternal life; indeed, He is "Life itself." He was there in the beginning and everything was made through Him. At the same time, He is the Savior of the world. Jesus Christ is both Creator and Savior of the universe.

When John wrote his Gospel, the Christian community was spreading rapidly among the Gentiles. The Jews from the very beginning — right after the Resurrection — began to expel the fledgling group of Jesus' followers from the synagogue and persecute them, hailing them before the Sanhedrin and often before the civil courts. Christians were persecuted because of their belief in Jesus as the Messiah, the anointed one of God, who had come to bring salvation to the whole world. The weak, the blind, the sick, women and children, are all included in His work of salvation. He made it clear that every person has a place in the mansions of the heavenly Father. It was impossible for Jesus, true God and true man, to limit His work to the Jewish community. His was an all-encompassing mission to all the peoples of the earth.

Fountain of life and Savior of the world, Christ is the object of faith. Every person is invited to have faith in Him. Faith, a dominant theme in the Gospel of John, is the ultimate human response to Jesus' person and mission. The Letter to the Hebrews (11:1) defines faith as "confidence in what's hoped for, conviction about things that can't be seen." The Gospel makes it clear that this faith is the primary condition of salvation. Believing in Jesus means recognizing the special relationship He has with the Father and the implications that has for us, namely the need to enter into a lifelong relationship with Christ that will lead us to the Father through the Holy Spirit. Faith, in the Gospel of John, is Trinitarian.

John's Gospel was addressed to a community in turmoil over the identity of Jesus. Some had been disciples of John the Baptist, others had been expelled from the Jewish community because of their belief in Jesus as the Messiah, and still others found it hard to believe that Jesus is God "in the flesh." Because of the constant confusion surrounding Jesus' identity, the community found itself divided into various factions and groups. The Gospel of John took shape in this hostile environment of the expanding Church in 90 A.D.

John defends Jesus' claim to be one with God Whom He calls "Father." That claim was confirmed by the signs He was able to perform. The miracles of Jesus corroborate His identity. John's Gospel presents Jesus announcing a new creation. The Bible starts with the words: "In the beginning God created the heaven and the earth" (Gn 1:1). John opens his Gospel: "In the beginning was the Word and the Word was with God and the Word was God" (Jn 1:1). If the old creation sinned and brought death and destruction to the world, God's goodness is manifested through the work of Christ Who restores all to its original beauty in a new creation.

The first sign of this new creation is the miracle at Cana in Galilee where Jesus transformed water into wine. This transformation indicates that the old times are gone and now humanity lives in the new time, the time of the Messiah. The Old Adam of sin is replaced by the New Adam (Jesus) of grace and salvation. Mary, the Mother of Jesus, is present when the New Adam accomplishes His first sign; she is the New Eve. It is not just a coincidence that John's Gospel, the Gospel of the New Creation, refers to Jesus as "the Man" (Jn 19:5) and Mary as "the Woman" (Jn 2:4 and 19:26). Jesus and Mary are what God exactly wanted man and woman to be from the beginning.

In a context of a serious theology, John describes several encounters between Jesus and women. To understand the nature and the implications of these encounters, we should keep in mind all the themes we have just developed: the identity of Jesus as God; His activity creating all things anew; the people's response of faith; and the hostile character of the religious factions of the time.

A Radical Change in the Life of a Samaritan Woman

The Gospel of John reports:

> He [Jesus] had to pass through Samaria, and he came to a Samaritan city named Sychar, near the field Jacob gave to his son Joseph. Now Jacob's well was there. So Jesus, tired out from the journey, simply sat down at the well. It was about noon.[2]

Galilee, where Jesus performed most of His ministry, is situated in the northern part of the Holy Land. The Sea of Galilee, the city of Capernaum (Peter's hometown), and the other sites around the lake are the familiar places where Jesus preached and healed. Judea is the area around Jerusalem and Bethlehem where Jesus often traveled. It was here, in the Temple of Jerusalem, that He often confronted the scribes and the Pharisees. Samaria is located between the two, at the center of the Holy Land.

Because of His frequent travels back and forth from Galilee to Judea, Jesus would often pass through Samaria. Jews often went around Samaria by taking an eastern route that followed the Jordan. They did not care to mingle with the Samaritans because they considered them unclean. In the eyes of the Jews, the Samaritans — who had declared their independence from Jerusalem and established their own place of worship — were an illegitimate sect no better than the pagans with whom they had intermarried. The Samaritans had their own temple for worship and their own religious calendar, different from the Jews.

116

Conflicts between the Samaritans and the Jews grew very strong. They disliked each other to the point of hatred. The Jews considered themselves to be the only rightful heirs to the Covenant and despised the practices of the Samaritans, considering them stupid and unworthy of God's covenant. In the heat of a controversy with a group of Jews in Jerusalem, Jesus was once accused of being a Samaritan.

If Jews chose to bypass Samaria, why would Jesus decide to go through that land? Why would John say that Jesus "had to pass through Samaria"? Jesus insisted on passing through Samaria not because of geographical, but because of theological necessity. As we shall see, Christ was on a mission to change a woman's life forever.

John mentioned the exact location in order to offer the reader the context in which the encounter took place between Jesus and the Samaritan woman. The site is significant because of the well that Jacob gave his son Joseph. It is an important place for the Jews in general because Jacob and Joseph represent the original unity of the people of the Covenant. Abraham, Isaac, Jacob and Joseph are the patriarchs of Israel who guaranteed that all their descendants would inherit God's promises to Israel. At the time of these patriarchs the divergence between the Jews and the Samaritans was centuries in the future.

If Jesus was not tired, He would not have stopped to rest at the well. In fact, the well is the public place where women gather to draw water and share what is happening in their lives and the life of the village. It is a place of meeting, like a mall or a park. Men did not feel comfortable at a well mingling with the women. But Jesus had no such qualms. Tired and thirsty after hours of dusty hiking, He did what most of us would do. He sat down at the well.

Describing Jesus as tired, John emphasizes the humanity of the Lord. He invites the reader to realize that Jesus was not a super human. He got tired like all of us because He was totally, completely, and fully human as much as He was totally, completely, and fully divine. The human qualities of Jesus do not, however, diminish His divinity or the divine character of His mission. Rather, His humanity expresses the humble nature of the Incarnation: Jesus truly became human, although He is divine by nature. Jesus is one with us in His humanity and one with the Father in His divinity.

Thus John's Gospel has set the scene in an accurately detailed historical framework. What happened there is a true event. We know where Jesus was: in a town of Samaria. We know exactly where He was, what the name of the town was, even what hour it was, noontime. The Jews thought of noon as the time of temptation. During the heat of the day, people get tired and it is easy for the devil to tempt them in all kinds of ways.

When Jesus was sitting at the well, "a Samaritan woman came to draw water. Jesus said to her, 'Give me a drink' — his disciples had gone off to the city to buy food" (Jn 4:7-8). As in many other situations, Jesus takes the initiative to begin the conversation. He surely knew that talking to a Samaritan woman would present three major problems for Him: first, she is a Samaritan; second, she is a woman; and third, He is alone with her because the disciples had gone into the city to buy some food.

Jesus should not be talking to this Samaritan woman because in doing so He is exposing Himself to ritual uncleanness. Her being a woman makes the situation even worse. Men do not publicly engage in a lengthy conversation with women, even if both are Jews. How can Jesus speak alone to a woman in such a public place where other women could show up at the well and see them talking together? But Jesus did it anyway, showing that public opinion did not shape His conduct. Why did He do it?

We are not the only ones asking this question. The Samaritan woman herself asked Him: "How is it that you, a Jew, ask me, a Samaritan woman, for a drink? — Jews don't associate with Samaritans" (Jn 4:9). It is hard for us to understand how big a problem it was for Jews to mingle with Samaritans in Jesus' time. The Samaritan woman herself was obviously shocked. Jews considered

Samaritans as ritually impure, and therefore Jews were forbidden to drink from any vessel they had handled.

Jesus' initiative in asking for a drink would have been unprecedented since giving Him water would imply a forbidden familiarity, something that the Samaritan woman herself was trying to avoid. She knew that giving Jesus water would start people gossiping. From her response, it is obvious that she did not want to talk to Jesus. But Jesus wanted to show that God is interested in the salvation of all people regardless of their social and religious background. And you'll notice that He does not manipulate the circumstances of this saving encounter. Rather, it is in a very normal situation that Jesus, tired and thirsty, asks this woman who was drawing water at a well to give Him a drink. He used this ordinary opportunity in order to convey God's message of love and concern to this woman.

Jesus says to her: "If you knew the gift of God and who it is who's saying to you, 'Give me a drink,' you would have asked him and he would have given you living water" (Jn 4:10). This is very hard to comprehend. The Samaritan woman asked a simple question about why Jesus was talking to her, and his answer brings the entire conversation up to another level. All of a sudden God is brought into the scene and Jesus puts Himself in relationship with God as part of Who he is. At first, it sounds as if Jesus is telling her that He is a "big shot." He is saying something like "If you knew Who I am, you would have given me water already. Actually, you would have asked me to give you water."

As we mentioned before in the Introduction, Jesus uses every encounter with people to reveal to them more clearly His identity. Up to this point, the Samaritan woman does not know what Jesus means by "the gift of God" and "Who Jesus is." In His longest conversation ever reported in the Gospels, Jesus uses a "divine" tactic in order to reveal to the woman His identity and God's gift to her and the world. This tactic does not seem "reasonable" if measured by human standards. In fact, it is amazing that Jesus would begin by immediately talking about God's gift to a Samaritan woman who was merely asking Him the reason behind His request for a drink of water.

In a variety of different situations, Jesus approaches people in such a way as to focus their attention on His message and His person and challenges them to think more deeply. Here He challenges the Samaritan woman by inviting God into her thoughts and by insinuating that He is different from the average man she meets every day. Although Jesus has already moved to the spiritual plane, claiming His power to provide the woman with "living water," she is still thinking about the water she has to draw from the well each day. Jesus does not explain immediately what He means by "living water." She is probably thinking that He knows of some "flowing water" that would be much more desirable than the stagnant water of the cistern.

The woman, unaware of where the conversation is going, asked Jesus: "Lord, you have no bucket and the well is deep, so where do you get the living water from? Surely you're not greater than our father Jacob who gave us the well and drank from it himself, as well as his sons and his herds?" (Jn 4:11-12).

The Samaritan woman is now paying more attention to Jesus because she addresses Him as "Lord," the Greek term (*Kyrie*) for "Master" which is a respectful mode of address for either a human being or a deity in the ancient Greek world. Although this was just the second time the woman had replied to Jesus' comment, her attitude has already reached a different level. She is interested now in what Jesus has to say and she becomes the one asking Him how can He get this "living water" if He doesn't have a bucket. Does Jesus think He is more important than Jacob who gave this cistern to his children and his flock?

It is obvious also that the woman is talking about the historical origin of the well, indicating that one of the patriarchs of the Jewish people, Jacob, had dug this well in order to give water to his children and his flock when they needed it. With God's help, Jacob was able to save them all from dying of thirst. It does not seem thus far that the woman has any idea what Jesus is talking about. If He is able to provide a "flowing water," then Jesus is certainly greater than Jacob who was able to provide only a cistern of stagnant water. In other words, the woman is now asking Jesus "Who are you? And what can you do to show me that you are greater than the patriarch, Jacob?"

Jesus answers her: "Everyone who drinks this water will thirst again. But whoever drinks the water I'll give him will never thirst; instead the water I'll give him will become in him a spring of water welling up in him to eternal life" (Jn 4:13-14). In saying this, Jesus unveils the spiritual meaning behind His use of the term "living water." Thus He draws a parallel between the physical water that Jacob provided in the Old Testament and the spiritual water that He would provide in the New. The relationship between these waters is like the relationship between shadow and reality. What the physical water does externally, the spiritual water does internally. Natural water refreshes the body and ensures continuity of physical life; spiritual water refreshes the soul and provides eternal life.

Jacob's well in the Old Testament is the symbolic reflection of the New Testament. The Old Covenant, although it provided water for the people of God, was still only a preparation for the true living water that would be given only by and through Christ to the world. Everybody who drinks of the physical water will thirst again; the water Christ gives is a spring of water welling up to eternal life. Even the water of Jacob, given him by God as a sign of recognition of his faith, is not enough and cannot substitute for Christ's living water.

Although the Samaritan woman started to express some curiosity about this, she was not ready yet to understand the spiritual depth of Jesus' words. He is talking about a "living water" that will give eternal life; she is still interested in water of better quality than what is in the cistern. She is being introduced to a different level of thinking; yet, she is struggling with the spiritual notion of "living water." She says to Jesus: "Lord, give me this water, so I won't become thirsty and won't have to come over here to draw water" (Jn 4:15).

Does her answer show that she perceives the deep insight of Jesus' expression? On one hand, she says that she needs living water so that she will not be thirsty anymore; on the other, she believes that she will not have to come to the well anymore if Jesus gives her the living water. Is she still concentrating on the literal meaning of water? The question remains.

Jesus shifted the conversation and said to the Samaritan woman: "'Go call your husband and come here.' The woman answered and said to him, 'I don't have a husband.' Jesus said to her, 'You were right when you said, "I don't have a husband" — you've had five men and the one you have now isn't your husband. You've spoken the truth'" (Jn 4:16-18). Why does Jesus ask the woman to go and call her husband? Is He afraid of what the people of the town will say if they see Him talking to a woman? Obviously not, because He already has been talking to her for quite a while now. Something else is meant here.

Husband and wife constitute a unity; they supplement each other. A husband in the Mediterranean culture of Jesus heads the family name and a wife completes him, finding her identity in and through him. It was expected that all people get married in that place and time, because society valued marriage highly. Since Jesus knew that the man living with the Samaritan woman was not her husband, His request to "go call your husband," was sort of a rhetorical question to demonstrate to her what He knew about her life.

It is notable that Jesus has a supernatural knowledge, especially in the Gospel according to Saint John. Here we find evidence of this supernatural power. Jesus is able to tell the woman something only she could have known about herself because of Who He was. Since John emphasizes Jesus' divinity, it is obvious that His divine identity is the answer. Divinity in Jesus does not deny or diminish His full and authentic humanity, nor does being totally and completely human ever obscure His divine character. Although acting with a human nature, Jesus is still the divine subject of His actions. The actions are being performed by a human nature, but they are still the actions of God. This constitutes the mystery of Christ's Incarnation in which humanity and divinity were united.

Jesus did not use the supernatural knowledge to show off, but only to lead the Samaritan woman to faith in Him. By confirming His knowledge of her situation, Jesus has her full attention. She says to Him: "'Lord, I see that you're a prophet. Our fathers worshipped on this mountain but you say that in Jerusalem is the Place where we should worship.' Jesus said to her, 'Believe me, woman, the hour is coming when you'll worship the Father neither on this mountain nor in Jerusalem. You worship what you don't know; we worship what we know, because salvation is from the Jews. But the hour is coming, and is now, when the true worshippers will worship the Father in spirit and truth, for indeed the Father seeks such people to worship Him. God is spirit, and those who worship Him must worship in spirit and truth'" (Jn 4:19-24).

The Samaritan woman addressed Jesus as "prophet" because He told her things about her life that He could not have naturally known. How could a Jew traveling through Samaria know so many secret things about her life? Subsequently, she becomes the one developing the theme of religion and worship. She refers to Gerizim, the mountain on which a temple was erected in the fourth century B.C. by Samaritans to rival Mount Zion where Jews worshiped God in the Temple of Jerusalem.

The Samaritan woman acknowledged the difference in religious traditions between the Jews and the Samaritans. She knows that these groups despised each other's religious practices. Talking to Jesus about the right way to worship God could open an endless argument. She began the subject because she was amazed at Jesus' knowledge of her life and because she sensed that He was a "prophet." The fact that she is beginning to think Jesus is on the right track of worship has her confused: If my way is the right way, how is it possible that a Jew is a "prophet" and knows the secrets of my life?

The answer Jesus gave the Samaritan woman regarding the nature of worship is universal. He discusses whether a "place" is important in worshiping God. Jesus never denied the essential role a place plays in the person's life of prayer. He himself frequented the synagogue on a weekly basis and often went to Jerusalem for the feast of Passover and prayed with His people in the Temple. This Temple was erected by David and rebuilt by Solomon as God's house where God had promised to abide forever. The importance of God's house as a place of worship and adoration is quite obvious in the Psalms.

In their religious practices the Jews thought it impossible to worship God outside the Temple of Jerusalem. The Temple was the heart and soul of the People of the Covenant; the place where the God of Israel was to be adored. It was the center of the Jewish religion. Every year Jews went to Jerusalem to celebrate the feast of Passover in the Temple. In a word, the identity of the Jewish people was totally connected with the Temple of Jerusalem on Mount Zion.

Over the centuries the Jews arrived at the conclusion that the Temple was the exclusive place of worship. They emphasized this kind of adoration to the point of excluding any other. Jesus does not abolish the Jewish religious practice of worshiping God in the Temple; He extends it to all places and elevates it to a totally different level, the level of the Spirit. He says to the Samaritan woman that the hour is coming "when you'll worship the Father neither on this mountain nor in Jerusalem" (Jn 4:21).

This totally unexpected statement must have confused the Samaritan woman. For us today it is very understandable for one to seek God everywhere. For the Jews of Jesus' time, however, it was absolutely unthinkable for a Jew to worship God while forgetting the centrality of the Jerusalem Temple. Jewish spirituality was connected to the city of Zion, God's city.

124

Jesus inaugurates a different type of worship: adoring the Father not necessarily connected to a place. The time is ripe for this new universal type of adoration to start; the new "space" for this adoration is also ready. The time is here because of Jesus' presence now in history; the space is the spirit of every believing person: "The hour is coming, and is now, when the true worshippers will worship the Father in spirit and in truth, for indeed the Father seeks such people to worship Him. God is spirit, and those who worship Him must worship in spirit and truth."

Jesus revealed to the Samaritan woman that the time had come for the true worshipers to worship the Father in Spirit and in truth. God is not a body of rules and laws as many Jews misunderstood. God is not bound by the letter of the Law, because God is Spirit. Although Jesus did not attempt to abolish the Jewish Law, He confirmed the supremacy of God's Spirit over the letter of the Law. In fact, the only reason for the Jewish Law to exist is its spirit, not its letter.

The time had come to bring the worship of the Jews to a new level; the letter of the Jewish Law is replaced by the spirit behind it. God is Spirit and those who worship Him should worship Him in Spirit. No single place could possibly be an exclusive location for worshiping God. The Spirit of God embraces all of creation, enabling every person to worship God always and everywhere. The Spirit is not contained in any space and so all those who approach God through the Spirit will worship God any time and anywhere.

The Spirit given by God reveals the truth about God and all of creation. This truth enables us to worship God appropriately. The Gospel of John describes Jesus as the bearer of the Spirit. Jesus communicates God's Spirit to all and, consequently, the Spirit "helps us in our weakness, for we don't know how to pray as we should" (Rm 8:26). The Spirit pleads for us in the way God desires that we worship.

The Samaritan woman was aware that the true way of worshiping God was to be revealed by the Messiah. She says to Jesus:

"'I know that the Messiah is coming, who is called the Anointed; when he comes, he'll tell us everything.' Jesus said to her, 'I who am speaking to you am he'" (Jn 4:25-26).

Among all the references in the New Testament, this is the strongest admission on the part of Jesus that He is, indeed, the Messiah, the Christ, the Anointed One, Who is to deliver God's people from their sins. While Jesus was always careful with the Jews, He did not hesitate to reveal to the Samaritan woman that He was the Christ. The Jews were expecting a certain type of Messiah and were not open to the idea of a Messiah Who did not fit their expectations.

Samaritans did not expect a Messianic King of the house of David; instead they expected a prophet like Moses (See Dt 18:15). According to the Samaritans' understanding, the Messiah was not going to be a Savior-King and a deliverer of God's people. The Samaritan woman, on the other hand, was open to any kind of Messiah sent by God. She says to Jesus that when the Christ comes, He will tell everybody everything. The only thing she knows is that the Christ will ultimately provide for unity among the people of the Covenant, and will lead them into the way of true and authentic worship.

Jesus' revelation of His identity to the Samaritan woman affected her life in a profound way. The sole reason Jesus had been talking to her was to convert her to believe in Him as the Christ. Why should she believe? Because her faith would change her life forever. Her salvation was the only thing Jesus had in mind when He opened a dialogue with her. At the height of the conversation with Him, the Samaritan woman realizes Who Jesus is and this changes everything. Suddenly she became His missionary. She ran into the town and told the people to "come see a man who told me everything I've done! Could this be the Messiah?" (Jn 4:29).

From the words of the Samaritan woman, it seems that the conversation she had with Jesus was long enough to make her feel that He knew everything about her. It could also be that she was exaggerating; Jesus told her certain essential things about her life, which to her, felt like everything. In any case, the meeting with Jesus totally amazed the Samaritan woman. The tactic Jesus used in drawing her step by step to discover His identity changed her life and led her to believe in Him.

The mission of the Samaritan woman was a success as John reports: "Many of the Samaritans from that city believed in him, based upon the word of the woman who bore witness that, 'He told me everything I've done!'" (Jn 4:39). She is described in virtually the same words as the disciples are in Jesus' prayer (see Jn 17:20). Was her role as a disciple and missionary to the Samaritan people of her town an easy one? Of course not. First, the Samaritans were not at all disposed to accept any Jewish teacher, even one claiming to be the Christ. Second, the Samaritan woman was obviously known in her own town as a sinner since she already had five men and the one living with her now was not her husband. It seems, therefore, that there must have been something very convincing in her words that aroused the people's curiosity about Jesus.

The work of the Samaritan woman was to draw their attention to Jesus. Once her job was done, the Samaritans wanted to discover for themselves the identity of Jesus:

> So when the Samaritans came to him they asked him
> to stay with them, and he stayed there for two days. And
> far more believed based upon his word, and they said
> to the woman, "No longer do we believe because of what
> you said — we've heard for ourselves and we know that
> this man is truly the savior of the world."[3]

Jesus stayed in Samaria for two full days. It was unthinkable for Samaritans to offer a Jewish teacher that kind of hospitality. They even invited Him to prolong His visit. We do not know what Jesus taught them and what kind of questions they asked. We do know, however, the awesome results of His preaching: many more began to believe in Him because of His word. They told the Samaritan woman that they now believed, not because of her testimony anymore, but because they heard for themselves. The result is beyond anyone's expectation: the Samaritans reported that they "know that this man is truly the savior of the world."

The Jewish leaders often accused Jesus of being possessed by demons. On several occasions, they wanted to seize Him and put Him to death because He claimed that God was Abba, His Father. He said that He Himself has always existed, even before Abraham, and He accused them, who claimed to be Abraham's children, of being the children of the devil. They refused to accept Jesus and denied any claim He made to His divine identity and His mission from the Father.

Unlike these contacts with the Jews, Jesus' mission to the Samaritans was a major success. The Samaritan woman was the instrument for Jesus' success. It is interesting to note that the longest conversation Jesus had in the Gospels is this one with the Samaritan woman. It was a truly meaningful encounter in which Jesus revealed His identity to her and through her attracted other people to believe in Him. Can we converse at length this way with today's modern woman?

The social setting is very different today. Life is more hectic. People would not be apt to engage in a lengthy conversation with a perfect stranger about personal matters, and they would be even less likely to invite him into their homes for a couple of days. One thing, however, guarantees continuity between the then and the now: the identity of a woman. Every woman lives with the struggle of discovering who she is. Her questions about the meaning of her existence reflect the serious nature of her reflections in this area. Fear, anxiety, and concern regarding her own existence and identity are not answered by technology. Modern discoveries that make us comfortable cannot provide the timeless self-knowledge that we need for real meaning and self-esteem in life.

The Samaritan woman invites every woman, no matter how inadequate she feels, to discover herself as she converses in her heart with Christ. The first step is to somehow make contact with Christ. The Samaritan woman did not ignore Him when He tried to talk to her. Instead, she answered His question, although she knew she was not supposed to talk to Him publicly. She overcame her social fear and opened a dialogue with Him. This fear of communicating with Christ is strangely very common today. It is easier to ignore Him, even though women realize they need something more than what they already have: a meaningful conversation with the Lord about their lives.

When women come to realize that they must live in and for Christ, they will be uneasy if they feel His absence for even a short period of time in their lives. Christ is a sweet companion and a God of salvation. No matter how much a contemporary woman may feel fulfilled by her social life, her comfortable lifestyle, and her friends, only Christ can give her a full appreciation of who she is and how much she means to God. Remember the Samaritan woman who, despite her sinful life, was inspired by Jesus to go and tell the townspeople that she talked to a man openly who told her everything about her life.

The second step is to ask Jesus questions because He respects our search for self-knowledge and our freedom. Our questions have to be sincere just like the questions of the Samaritan woman who asked Jesus: why are you talking to me? Every woman has the right to say to Jesus: why are talking to me? Jesus respects our sincerity in seeking to understand the reason behind His presence in our lives. The most important factor in our conversation with Jesus is the freedom we have in allowing Christ to come into our lives. The Samaritan woman had full freedom to reject Jesus' request for a drink of water. Her questioning of the reason behind his conversation is valid because it shows that, even in our relationship with God, we do not become robots. We maintain our freedom, even when the Lord invites us to follow as He opens a conversation with us.

Jesus enjoys listening to the longings of human hearts. Women have thousands of questions they want to ask Jesus, but they oftentimes do not take the initiative to do so because they are fearful of what society might think of them. Some women live for years a life full of pain and anxiety without taking their problems to Jesus. Rather, they choose to allow society to tell them what to think and do.

In Scripture, the long dialogue between Jesus and the Samaritan woman conveys a strong message: Jesus wants to have a deep conversation with every woman. He wants to liberate her from the limitations of her workaday life and open her heart to the eternal treasures of living water. He grants His living water to every woman who asks Him for it and is interested in His identity and mission.

More than ever before, there is a strong longing in women's hearts to know who they are, how they can experience a fuller, more abundant life, and how to have a more fruitful, loving relationship with others. What many women do not know is that the fulfillment they seek is to be found in Christ Who is always ready to receive and never reject them because His ultimate goal is to grant them eternal life in abundance. St. John's major theme of a "new creation" applies to the Samaritan woman and to every woman who ever existed. Christ transforms the woman who come to Him into a new creation, maintaining her identity as a woman and as a person, but changing her being into one that lives in and through Him. At the beginning of creation, Eve sinned against God (Genesis 1 and 2); in the Gospel of John, the Samaritan woman (and every woman) turns her back on sin and follows the words of Christ. She is a "new creation."

To be a "new creation" means to be totally immersed in Christ. The change that women experience is a burning desire to live and breath Christ's word of salvation. Those women who have discovered this word and live by it are saddened by the fact that so many of their sisters are missing the joy of knowing and being with Christ. Conversing with the Lord has become "a spring of water welling up in him to eternal life" (Jn 4:14) and they want others to join in the discussion and reap the benefits that Christ has to offer.

Face to Face with the Evil of Adultery: Jesus Sides with the Adulterous Woman

Saint John is the only Evangelist who reports the story of a woman caught in adultery. He says:

> Early in the morning he [Jesus] again came to the Temple and all the people came to him, and after taking a seat he began to teach them. Then the scribes and the Pharisees brought a woman who had been caught in adultery, and after standing her out in the middle they said to him, "Teacher, this woman was caught in the act of adultery. Now in the Torah Moses commanded us to stone such women. So what do *you* say?" They said this to test him, so they would have something to accuse him of. But Jesus bent down and began to write on the ground with his finger. When they kept asking him, he straightened up and said to them, "Let whoever is without sin among you be the first to throw a stone at her." And once again he bent down and began to write on the ground. Then those who had been listening began to go away, one by one, beginning with the elders, and he was left alone, with the woman still in the middle. Jesus straightened up and said to her, "Woman, where are they? Has no one condemned you?" "No one, Lord," she said. Then Jesus said, "Neither do I condemn you. Go your way, and from now on sin no more."[4]

This story is unique because it took place in the Temple after Jesus spent all night praying on the Mount of Olives. This mountain is not mentioned elsewhere in the Gospel tradition except during Passion Week. It is a special place because Jesus went there regularly with His disciples (Lk 22:39). He was able to find shelter and a place to rest on the Mount of Olives far from the bustling crowd. On many occasions Jesus would spend the night on this Mount talking with His heavenly Father. On the eve of His death, He went there to pray and was captured by the Roman soldiers.

It was very convenient for Him that the Mount of Olives is situated right outside the city of Jerusalem. That night Jesus prayed at length to His heavenly Father and early in the morning "he again came to the Temple and all the people came to him, and after taking a seat he began to teach them" (Jn 8:2). The Temple was the religious, spiritual, cultural, and even social center of the Jewish religion. People met in the Temple of Jerusalem not only to pray, but also to find out what was going on in the Jewish world. The Temple provided a sense of belonging for every Jew and constituted the true center of their daily activity in Jerusalem.

The scribes and Pharisees played a fundamental role in teaching all those who came to the Temple. People looked up to them and considered them authentic teachers of God's Law. They were respected and obeyed, although they often did not practice what they taught. They prided themselves on the role of teacher and did not like the fact that Jesus also taught the people in the Temple. John's Gospel presents a series of controversies between Jesus and the Jews taking place in the Temple.

Jesus tried to interpret Scriptures the way God intended them to be understood. His way of perceiving God's Law constantly challenged the authority of the scribes and Pharisees as teachers. Despite the controversy surrounding His teaching, Jesus grew in popularity: "All the people came to him," a fact that stirred the jealousy of the Jewish leaders. Jesus became for the people an authority figure commanding the attention of many who came to the Temple.

His popularity was a challenge to the Jewish leaders who sought ways to discredit Him. And so it happened on one occasion that "the scribes and the Pharisees brought a woman who had been caught in adultery, and after standing her out in the middle" (Jn 8:3) asked Jesus to judge her. The Fourth Commandment, "Do not commit adultery," was addressed by God to the entire Jewish nation, men and women alike. Where are the men who slept with this woman? Why aren't they also standing "in the middle" with her? How can the scribes and Pharisees justify this double standard which treated men so leniently but insisted on stoning a woman for committing adultery? Where is God's mercy in all this? Did they really expect Jesus to agree with them?

"Teacher," they said, "this woman was caught in the act of adultery. Now in the Torah Moses commanded us to stone such women. So what do *you* say?" (Jn 8:4-5). In fact, not unlike the Shariah law found in some fundamentalist Muslim countries today, the Book of Deuteronomy prescribed the stoning of a betrothed virgin who had committed adultery (see Dt 22:23-24). Jesus had publicly said that He had come, not to abolish the Law, but to fulfill it. On the other hand, Jesus' compassion and love for sinners was likewise well known. What a perfect opportunity to trap Him. Indeed, "they said this to test him, so they would have something to accuse him of" (Jn 8:6).

It looks like the Pharisees and the scribes were not concerned about justice or what God's will in the matter might be. They had no real interest in the fate of this woman. The spirit of the Law never occurred to them. All they cared about was that here they had an opportunity to discredit Jesus.

If He were to say they should not stone her, He would be contradicting the letter of the Law which He claimed to have come to fulfill. The Law of Moses was inspired by God, but the spirit behind it was not well understood. Jesus came to reveal the ultimate purpose behind God's Law: to promote perfect love of God and neighbor.

Jesus did not immediately answer the question of the Jewish leaders. Instead, He bent down and started tracing something in the sand. Why was Jesus writing on the ground and what did He write? The Prophet Jeremiah says: "Those who turn away from You shall be written in the earth, for they have forsaken the Lord, the fountain of living water" (Jr 17:13). Some Bible scholars think

133

that Jesus was writing the sins of the elders who wanted to stone the adulterous woman. This is, however, just an assumption. No one knows why and what Jesus was scribbling in the sand. What it was will remain known only to God forever.

Jesus' response to them was: "Let whoever is without sin among you be the first to throw a stone at her" (Jn 8:7). In the Book of Deuteronomy, the first stones were to be thrown by the very witnesses who caught the woman in the act of adultery. Jesus asks the Pharisees and the scribes if they thought they were sinless, then to throw the first stone at the woman. He stands between the sinful woman and the Jewish leaders and defends her by turning their judgment of her back on themselves. On another occasion, He had cautioned His listeners, "Don't judge, so that you won't be judged" (Mt 7:1). His action here shows God's love for the sinner. Against all human standards, God wants every person to be saved. It is in His forgiveness that God enables the sinner, through Jesus, to experience His undying love.

Jesus' action reveals the part that is missing in their interpretation of the Law of Moses, namely, the universal character of God's Law. Every person should abstain from adultery. In order to make themselves look holy, the Jewish leaders often pointed out the sins and weaknesses of others whom they considered to be the refuse of society. Jesus challenges their claim to be holier than everybody, and they quickly left the scene when Jesus asked them to throw the first stone at the woman.

This story is what we call a "biographical apothegm," in which Jesus' opponents set a "trap" from which He must escape through a wise instructive saying (see also, Mk 12:13-17, on the tribute coin; Mk 10:1-12, on the question of marriage and divorce). Jesus' logic outwitted those who had set a trap for Him. Even the crowd that had been watching departed. Aware of their own sins, all those who had come to judge the woman dropped their accusations and disappeared: "He was left alone, with the woman still in the middle" (Jn 8:9).

Behind the literal meaning of the statement "He was left alone, with the woman still in the middle," there is also a spiritual one. The God-man, Jesus Christ, is face-to-face with a sinful woman: He alone is capable of judging her with the mind and heart of God. He alone understood her situation thoroughly. If we want to read a little more into the text, each one of us will eventually stand alone before Jesus in the final judgment. We can be as grateful as the woman in this Gospel passage that Jesus, God in person, loves and forgives, heals and promotes a radical change of life.

Jesus does not deny that the woman's action was sinful. At the same time, He is disturbed that the scribes and Pharisees would set themselves up as her judges and that they would judge her so severely and without any mercy. "Jesus straightened up and said to her, 'Woman, where are they? Has no one condemned you?' 'No one, Lord,' she said. Then Jesus said, 'Neither do I condemn you. Go your way, and from now on sin no more'" (Jn 8:10-11). John's message is a powerful one: God did not send Jesus to condemn the world but to save the world. In this sense, Jesus says: "I judge no one" (Jn 8:15). After the accusers left, He makes it clear that He does not intend to condemn her. The woman is free to go but not to sin again.

This does not mean that Jesus will not judge the world. He already revealed that the Father has placed the world's judgment in His hands: "For the Father judges no one; instead He's given all judgment to the Son" (Jn 5:22). He also emphasizes, "But even if I do judge, my judgment is true, because I'm not alone; rather I and the Father Who sent me bear witness" (Jn 8:16). Jesus does not want to judge anybody in the sense of condemning them. His mission is to confirm God's infinite mercy toward the sinner. At the same time Jesus is very clear in showing God's radical rejection of evil. Great as God's mercy is on those who commit adultery, His rejection of sin is even greater. Jesus tells the woman that He does not condemn her; but He also said to her, "Go and sin no more."

Jesus does not want anyone to pass judgment on the woman.

He knows that it is very easy to get carried away and condemn others. While it is normal to evaluate a person's character from the point of view of their actions, it takes wisdom and strength to draw the line between judging a person and judging his or her actions. The correct way is to abstain from judging others and let God be the only One to do so. At the same time, we should never forget that Jesus' message to every sinner is: sin no more. We need to identify evil and condemn it, even though we are not allowed to judge the person who is doing it.

It is all too common a practice to judge others. Very few people in this world are living such a deep spirituality that they are able to abstain from judging others when they see them doing evil. How many women are judged every day for something they have done. They are called names and are despised by society. Why aren't the same norms applied to those men who commit the same actions and lead women to sin? Jesus' invitation for the adulterous woman to sin no more echoes throughout all generations. Fornication and adultery have always been a temptation for every human being. It is in our nature to desire to be with others in an intimate relationship. We all have sexual desires and find it often very hard to control them. People who yield to those disorderly desires end up "sleeping around" and often cheat on their legitimate partners. Sexual desires constitute a strong driving force in our human nature.

At the beginning of creation, God instilled sexuality in human nature as a gift to be used in an orderly fashion. He created man and woman for each other so that, through their mutual self-giving, they express God's union with humanity. Jesus revealed later on that the union between man and woman in marriage reflects Jesus' union with and love for the Church. Sexuality is therefore a great gift from God if it is used according to God's plan, not according to our inordinate desires.

Unfortunately, with humanity's fall into sin, men and women lost their original innocence and their sense of what God intended in the use of the gift of sexuality. Men and women have sexual relationships without being married to each other and wonder why their conscience is uneasy about what they are doing. Today, the greatest excuse for promiscuous sexual activity (including fornication and adultery) is that it is normal, or natural. Under the excuse that "everybody is doing it" people have fallen into the erroneous conviction that all sexual activity whether within or outside marriage is permissible. Today, a high school or a college student is considered abnormal if he or she opposes premarital sex. People resent being told, even by God Himself, what they can and cannot do. They strongly feel they know exactly what is good for them and subscribe to society's norms in the area of moral behavior.

The majority challenge God's authority in establishing the criteria for good and evil in this area. They do not think that God knows what is truly good or evil for us. By accepting what appears to them as good, they establish themselves as gods over their own life. The Gospel never tires of telling us, as is obvious from the story of the adulterous woman, that God reserves the right to identify what is truly good for us. Jesus told that woman not to commit adultery because it is not good for her. Whether she was earning her living in that way or not, He judges adultery as an evil to be avoided.

No person has the right to judge others. However, the Church is commissioned to preach God's moral Law and to urge people to follow it. This mission was entrusted by Christ to His Church. Abstaining from judging sinful persons themselves does not mean approval of sinful, evil acts. The Church can never condone an evil action no matter how much she cares for the sinner. But the judgment is reserved to God alone.

The Gospel asks for a radical commitment to an eternal truth, to which we are all bound. The truth is that every act of adultery is a serious sin. What answer can we offer those who claim that there is love behind that sexual act? Love alone cannot justify a sexual act.

I once had a conversation with a young woman. She was claiming that love justifies sex. I asked her: if she was in love with her husband and another man came into her life, would she have a sexual relationship with the other man? She answered yes, if there was true love. Then I asked her again: now that you are in love with the second man, what if a third man came into your life, would you have sex with him too? Her answer was positive again, with the condition that there was true love between them. I persisted with a fourth and a fifth man until the fiftieth. At a certain point she had to say no because I think she must have realized that those who were listening to us felt that her lifestyle was devoid of any commitment at all.

While I think I made my point, I don't think I changed her mindset that multiple sexual partners are justified if love is involved. There are many people who subscribe to this loose morality, which is certainly not a message they learn from the Word of God.

What if you fall in love with a married person and really love them, are you allowed to have a sexual relationship with them? The answer is obvious. No. However, if you claim "love justifies sex," then you hold that you can have sex with that person. Ultimately, this logic will lead to absurdity because it is impossible to justify a sexual activity based solely on the motive of love. Love is a decision that involves the will, not mere emotional or physical attraction.

Jesus clearly teaches us that sexual activity should take place only in the context of marriage. Marriage is the institution where one man and one woman mutually offer themselves to each other in an awesome expression of love. This was the way God established it; every other way contradicts God's plan and wisdom.

Jesus addresses every woman of today inviting her not to sin in this regard. He wants her to realize the dignity she has in His eyes and the important role her body plays in her existence. Both men and women too easily allow themselves to engage in sexual activities. Some even brag about their adventures and how good and pleasurable the sexual experience was. Worse still is the fact that even good families are beginning to accept these things as normal. They often accuse the Church of "not being realistic" in dealing with the question of sexuality.

The Church is aware of the thinking patterns of the day and what is taking place in the field of sexual relationships. However, the Church does not believe that sex should be considered mere entertainment. It should never lose its private character and its purpose in our society. The Church defends the dignity of the person by proclaiming that sex should remain an intimate, private, holy and committed relationship between one man and one woman in marriage. Jesus' invitation to the adulterous woman not to sin anymore will remain an invitation to all woman of all times. Those who try to do right will find a peaceful satisfaction in following the eternal and true Law of Christ.

The Resurrection from the Dead: Not a Dilemma for Martha

When Jesus learned that His friend Lazarus died, He went up to Bethany in order to raise him from the dead. John the Evangelist reports:

> Now Bethany was near Jerusalem, about two miles away, and many of the Jews had come to Martha and Mary to console them over their brother. So Martha, when she heard that Jesus was coming, met him, but Mary stayed at the house. Martha said to Jesus, "Lord, if you'd been here, my brother wouldn't have died! but even now I know that whatever you ask God for, God will give you." Jesus said to her, "Your brother will rise!" Martha said to him, "I know that he'll rise at the resurrection on the last day." Jesus said to her, "*I* am the resurrection and the life! Whoever believes in me, even if he should die, will live, and everyone who lives and be-

lieves in me shall never die. Do you believe this?" She said to him, "Yes, Lord, I've come to believe that you're the Messiah, the Son of God who has come into the world!"[5]

We mentioned earlier in our analysis of Mark's Gospel the support that friends and neighbors gave to the family of someone who passed away. When Lazarus died, a large number of people came from Jerusalem in order to comfort Mary and Martha. The presence of these friends and relatives from Jerusalem at the scene of Lazarus' resurrection provides a link to the Jerusalem authorities with whom Jesus often found Himself in conflict. These authorities were following all the stages of Jesus' ministry, mainly out of curiosity. Because Lazarus had been buried for four days, no one could question the fact that Lazarus had come back from death when Jesus called him forth from the tomb.

Martha was a very energetic person. When she heard that Jesus was on His way to visit her and her sister, she could not remain at home waiting. Instead, she went out to meet Him; but Mary sat at home. Jesus was a close friend of Lazarus and his sisters, a fact that immediately leads to friendly conversation. Because of this friendship, Martha must have been emotional in talking to Jesus, especially because she knew about Jesus' ability to perform a miracle that could have prevented her brother's death.

Martha says to Jesus: "Lord, if you'd been here, my brother wouldn't have died! But even now I know that whatever you ask God for, God will give you." She voices the common expectation that even the crowd has. One Who is well known for His miracles should have been able to heal Lazarus. The miracle would have been assured because Lazarus was a dear friend of the Lord. In fact, the only time the Gospel reports that Jesus wept is at Lazarus' tomb (Jn 11:35).

Jesus' controversies with the Jewish leaders were based on the fact that He was trying to convince them of His divine mission.

Jesus' ultimate claim was that the Father sent Him and that He was doing everything in and through the Father. Near the tomb of Lazarus were "many of the Jews" who had come from Jerusalem. Martha confesses a faith in Jesus that recognized God as the source of Jesus' power. It separates her from those in the crowd who are amazed by Jesus' deeds and divided over His identity.[6]

Martha had no doubt about Jesus and His mission. She was not questioning Who He might be. It is ironic that it is Martha — a woman, in the presence of those Jews who should have accepted Jesus' divine mission — who confesses her belief in the power of the Lord. Instead of male Pharisees and scribes teaching the people in the Temple in Jerusalem about the divine origin of Jesus' power, it is a woman who assumes the task and proclaims Jesus' supernatural authority in Bethany near the grave of her brother. Martha becomes the very first one to talk to Jesus publicly and in direct language proclaiming His divine mission through the miracles He has been performing.

Jesus said to Martha, "Your brother will rise." Jesus' words draw from Martha an expression of her belief in the eschatological resurrection of the dead (see also Jn 5:28-29 and 4:25) as she answers, "I know that he'll rise at the resurrection on the last day." Martha knew about Jesus' miracles and wished that He was there in order to prevent her brother's death. Jesus elevates the conversation to a level higher: the resurrection from the dead. He confirmed the resurrection of her brother. She answered that she believes that there will be resurrection on the last day.

Before John wrote his Gospel, Mark had already reported a controversy between Jesus and the Sadducees who did not believe in the final resurrection from the dead. Jesus answered their doubt in the resurrection by saying: "Isn't this the reason you go astray, that you understand neither the Scriptures nor the power of God?" Faith in the resurrection rests on faith in God Who "is not God of the dead but of the living."[7] The Letter of Saint Paul to the Romans confirms the resurrection from the dead as the work of the

Most Holy Trinity: "If the Spirit of God who raised Christ from the dead dwells within you, then the One Who raised Christ from the dead will give life to your dead bodies through His Spirit that dwells within you" (Rm 8:11).

But there is more. Jesus links faith in the resurrection to His own Person: "I am the resurrection and the life! Whoever believes in me, even if he should die, will live, and everyone who lives and believes in me shall never die!" These are the words Jesus uttered to Martha after she confessed her belief in the resurrection of the dead. It is Jesus Himself Who on the last day will raise up those who have believed in Him. He has already given a sign and pledge of this by restoring some of the dead to life (e.g., the daughter of Jairus, the son of the widow of Nain, and Lazarus).

By raising people from the dead, Jesus announces His own Resurrection, though it was to be of a fuller dimension. Without Jesus' Resurrection there would not be the much wider resurrection of all the dead. Because Jesus rose from the dead, He opened the door for every human person in history to be raised from the dead. At the end of time, God will raise all bodies from the tomb to share in Jesus' superabundant and eternal life. Jesus proclaims this great truth to Martha and invites all those listening to accept the wondrous belief in the resurrection of the human body.

Jesus' "I am" follows Martha's confession of faith. Already in chapter 8, Jesus told the Jews that before Abraham was, "I am." Jesus applies to Himself the name "I am," which means Yahweh, the God of Israel. The Person of Jesus Christ, God and man, is the Resurrection and the Life. As such, Jesus will communicate His risen life to all at the end of time.

The expressions "the Resurrection" and "the Life" are major themes in the Gospel of John. They indicate God's ultimate intervention in the life of every human person. They are the unfailing promise of surviving this frail human condition. Talking to Martha, Jesus reveals the secret of His identity: Jesus is the Life and the Resurrection in person. In the very heart of Judaism, Jesus pro-

142

claims His identity using direct language. Two miles outside of Jerusalem, Jesus brings full light to the confusion people had about His identity. What the scribes and Pharisees have been tortured about, now is being clearly declared: Jesus is the Messiah, the Son of God, the One Who is coming into the world.

As in most other instances, Jesus, after revealing to Martha Who He was, invites her to believe in Him. Martha's answer entails three parts. She says: "Yes, Lord. I've come to believe that you're the Messiah, the Son of God, who has come into the world." She proclaims Him Messiah, Son of God, and the One Who has come into the world. Her words do not point to what Jesus has just revealed, but to three Christological affirmations made in the Gospel of John. One of John's concerns in this Gospel is to affirm the divine identity of Jesus, which is clearly conferred through those titles.

As in the story of the Samaritan woman at the well, this conversation with Martha is also very profound. It entails revelations about the mystery of God, the human person, and the world. Martha earned Jesus' revelation by being His friend and by going forth "to meet Him." It was the longing of her human heart that moved Martha to take the initiative to welcome the Lord. While it may have been considered disrespectful to leave behind the mourning family and friends, Martha casts aside her society's taboos because honoring Jesus took precedence. His presence made her ignore all customs. Her curiosity and faith in Jesus prepared her to receive the deepest revelations about Jesus' Person.

It takes courage for today's women to go out of their way to meet Jesus. Christ is always there revealing the most secret mysteries of His Person; He invites all women to come to Him. The first step consists in taking the initiative by leaving everything behind and going to "meet the Lord." On many occasions this meeting will take place outside the ordinary routine of life. Just like Martha who left all human affairs behind her in order to meet Jesus outside of her house, women need to leave their usual "home" in order to meet Christ. I mean they need to go beyond the ordinary in order to meet the extraordinary. It takes courage, love, and an adventurous spirit to do this. On His part, Christ leads to perfection every woman who seeks Him with a determined will, a sincere heart, unwavering hope and true love.

Notes

[1] See Pheme Perkins, "The Gospel according to John," in *The New Jerome Biblical Commentary*, New Jersey: Prentice Hall, 1990, 945.

[2] Jn 4:4-6.

[3] Jn 4:40-42.

[4] Jn 8:1-11.

[5] Jn 11:18-27.

[6] See Pheme Perkins, "The Gospel according to John," in *The New Jerome Biblical Commentary*, New Jersey: Prentice Hall, 1990, 970.

[7] See Mk 12:24-27; *Catechism of the Catholic Church*, 993.

Bibliography

Buby, Bertrand. *Mary of Galilee, Vol. II: Woman of Israel - Daughter of Zion*, Staten Island, NY: Alba House, 1995.

Catechism of the Catholic Church, San Francisco, CA: Ignatius Press/Libreria Editrice Vaticana, 1994.

Congregation for the Doctrine of the Faith, Declaration *Inter Insigniores,* no. 6: AAS 69 (1977).

Flannery, Austin, ed. *Vatican Council II*, Boston, MA: St. Paul Books & Media, 1992.

Gustin, Marilyn. *Discovering God's Word*, California: Benziger Publishing Company, 1995.

Harrington, Daniel J. "The Gospel According to Mark," in *The New Jerome Biblical Commentary*, Princeton, NJ: Prentice Hall, 1990, 596-629.

Pope John Paul II. Apostolic Letter *Mulieris Dignitatem*, no. 27: AAS 80 (1988).

McBrien, Richard P. *Encyclopedia of Catholicism*. San Francisco, CA: HarperCollins Publishers, 1995.

Nachef, Antoine E. *Mary's Pope: John Paul II, Mary, and the Church since Vatican II*. WI: Sheed and Ward, 2000.

_____. *The Faith of Mary*. Staten Island, NY: Alba House, 2002.

Schaberg, Jane. "Thinking Back Through the Magdalene," in *Continuum* vol. 1, no. 2 (1991): 71-90.

The New Jerome Biblical Commentary. Princeton, NJ: Prentice Hall, 1990.

ST PAULS

This book was produced by St. Pauls/Alba House, the Society of St. Paul, an international religious congregation of priests and brothers dedicated to serving the Church through the communications media.

For information regarding this and associated ministries of the Pauline Family of Congregations, write to the Vocation Director, Society of St. Paul, P.O. Box 189, 9531 Akron-Canfield Road, Canfield, Ohio 44406-0189. Phone (330) 702-0359; or E-mail: spvocationoffice@aol.com or check our internet site, www.albahouse.org